The Other Side
of Death

The Other Side of Death

JAN PRICE

FAWCETT COLUMBINE • NEW YORK

A Fawcett Columbine Book
Published by Ballantine Books

Copyright © 1996 by Jan Price

Library of Congress Cataloging-in-Publication Data
Price, Jan.
The other side of death / Jan Price.
p.   cm.
ISBN 0-449-90992-1
1. Near-death experiences.   2. Price, Jan.   I. Title.
BF1045.N4P75 1996
133.9'01'3—dc20   95-31254
CIP

ISBN: 0-449-90992-1

Manufactured in the United States of America

First Edition: March 1996

10   9   8   7   6   5   4   3   2

To me.

To John.

To love.

To life.

Contents

Acknowledgments

My thank-you list is big and long, but to these special ones I am deeply grateful:

The man I live, laugh, and love with—my husband, John Randolph Price—for giving me his time and putting aside his own projects to organize all my little pieces of paper into a format for this book, for adding his own feelings and thoughts about our shared experience, for researching many reference books for needed data, and most of all for encouraging me to write it.

Melody Juarez and Carl Wengenroth, Kendall County EMS attendants, whose quick action and expertise prevented this from being a channeled book.

Laura Weaver and Jack Cooper, who literally took over all my duties at the office and cheered me on.

Susan and Leslie, daughters mine, for your love and inspiration.

Maggi, beloved four-footed friend, for being my teacher on both sides of the veil.

Thank you all!

The Other Side
of Death

1

Not an Ordinary
Kind of Day

Thursday, December 30, 1993

A very fortunate woman am I. Each morning someone turns on the classical music station, brings
two cups of hot black coffee to bed, then snuggles in
close with me to sip the brew and watch through the
bedroom window as the orangy-red sun majestically rises
over the green hills. That someone is John, a writer of
wonderful books and the man I've shared my life with
for more than forty years. Neat way to start a day.

December 30, 1993, was no different. Laughing and
talking in bed at six-thirty that morning, I couldn't have
imagined that in less than seven hours I would die.
Death can be very educational. I know that I learned a
lot about living by dying, and I would not trade that experience for anything. For anyone who has ever wondered, you do go somewhere when you die. If you didn't,
you couldn't come back, and I did. Aren't round-trip
tickets wonderful? But I'm getting ahead of myself.

We finished our coffee and jumped out of bed for a quick face wash, then dressed for a long walk down our country lane. We live a few miles north of Boerne, Texas—a small town in the hills near San Antonio. It was a beautiful morning, cool and clear, and I was looking forward to a good stretch of the legs and some deep breathing of the clean fresh air. Watching for cottontail bunnies to scoot across the road is fun too. I always feel that I've done something good when I see one— probably something my mother told me when I was a kid. There wasn't a rabbit in sight that morning. But a very strange thing did happen.

As we passed one house, a dog walked nonchalantly out of his yard and bit me on the leg. I was shocked. So was John. Dogs don't bite me; dogs love me. Why on earth would one do such a thing? After he sunk his teeth into my leg and made a hole in my favorite gray sweatpants, he casually turned around and went back into his yard. I think John yelled something at him, then asked me if I wanted to turn around and go home. "Yeah," I said, "I can feel the blood running down my leg."

Back at the house I cleaned and bandaged the wound and called the people who owned the dog so that I could be assured the dog's shots were up-to-date. They were, and the man said that his dog doesn't bite people. Uh-huh. Hanging up, I started to cry. I just sobbed because a dog bit me and I couldn't figure out why. I know that sounds silly. John probably thought so too, but he held me for a while and I felt better.

That done, I made us a breakfast of my special French toast. Afterward it seemed a good idea to have some quiet time before going to the office. I called to tell my colleagues about my traumatic experience with the dog and said I'd be in later. Then I began to feel funny. I wasn't sure what it was, but my body felt strange. Throughout the morning as I showered and dressed, talked on the phone (our daughter, Leslie, called from France for a spinach lasagna recipe), and made my to-do list for the day, that strange feeling ebbed and flowed. It was aggravating because I never feel bad, and I had a lot to do that day.

It was almost noon when I was finally ready to go, and I heated some soup so that I wouldn't have to stop for lunch later. One sip made me feel ill and I threw up. Then the pressure began to increase in my chest, and the backs of my arms started to ache. This was weird. I stretched out on the bed, but only felt worse. I sat up and it was no better, so I got up and walked around hugging myself, trying to decide what to do.

John came up from his study about then, and I told him what was happening. He wanted to call a doctor, and for lack of a better plan I said okay. The only problem was, we didn't have a doctor—so he got out the Yellow Pages and started down the list. Not a doctor anywhere; the recordings all said they were out to lunch. Finally John got a human voice that said the doctor would be back around one-thirty and suggested we call Kendall County EMS.

Well, that sounded pretty extreme, and I knew they

would probably take me to a hospital emergency room in San Antonio, which was the last thing I wanted to do. This was dumb. Why didn't it just go away?

John asked, "What do you want me to do, honey?" And I heard myself say, "I guess you'd better call EMS." He did, and then called our office. Laura, our administrative director, answered. John told her what was happening, and she immediately swung into action by activating a prayer network.

The record shows that John's call to the Kendall County Emergency Medical Service was received at 1:15, and the ambulance was dispatched at 1:25 with Melody Juarez and Carl Wengenroth on board. They would have left sooner, but regulations call for a response team of three people, so they decided to wait a few minutes for the other paramedic. But Carl, who was driving the ambulance, began to feel uneasy. He turned to Melody and said, "Something tells me that we've got to leave now!" She agreed, and told us later that if they had delayed any longer, the full arrest would have occurred before their arrival. I'm sure glad there were angels on the scene.

While we were waiting, John ran in and out of the house, checking on me and watching for the ambulance—in our rural area the house numbers aren't easy to find. I started to feel quite warm and changed clothes several times, unsure what to wear for EMS. I finally chose navy knit pants and a striped T-shirt. I'm not sure why, but I'm glad I picked that shirt because it was a fairly old one and ended up being cut off me when I arrived at the hospital.

Once dressed, I lay down on the bed, and though the pressure had intensified, I felt very calm—no concern, nothing seemed particularly important. I was distancing. John reported that he could hear the ambulance, then the siren stopped, and then they appeared in our driveway. The paramedics rolled a gurney into our house, to the entrance of our bedroom. Because of the furniture arrangement and the step down, they had to park it about five feet from the bed.

The pleasant face of a young woman peered down at me. That was Melody, who was in her late thirties with blond hair pulled back in a ponytail. She smiled and asked me what day it was, when I was born, and other similar questions while taking my pulse. "Your pulse is strong," she said.

"I'm glad," I said, "because my lips are numb."

"Can you walk to the gurney?"

"Yes." And I did.

Since it appeared they were going to take me away, I said to John, "Be sure to bring my purse"—I guess I thought I'd need to refresh my makeup later on. Then I remember saying, "I feel dizzy." Since things got a little fuzzy after that, I had to rely on Melody's EMS report for details:

Patient's pulse and respiration were taken. I advised patient we would place monitor [EKG] on her as soon as she was belted on stretcher. Patient walked to stretcher. . . . As patient was placed on stretcher, she advised she felt very dizzy and became unconscious, unresponsive, no pulse . . . patient was in V-Tach [very wide and fast ventricular rate] to V-Fib [ventricular fibrillation—blood flow to the heart stops completely] ... full arrest, no pulse ... precardial thump was applied, no change in pulse. Quick look still showed V-Fib [full arrest]. Patient shocked [electric paddles] at 200 J, no pulse. Patient shocked at 300 J, no pulse. Patient shocked at 360 J ... slow heartbeat ... patient's respiratory effort was assisted with [oxygen] ... regained respiratory rate rapidly after third shock and heart rate returned. She became semiconscious, pupils slightly dilated, did respond to daylight.

The EMS report also stated that Melody and Carl arrived on the scene at one-thirty, and in less than four minutes, I was belted down on the stretcher. As noted, I quickly lost consciousness—not a blackout as in a faint, but a complete detachment of the mental faculties from the physical system as it was shutting down. The death process was beginning. My breathing had stopped, and when Melody checked my pulse, she couldn't find one. The life force was withdrawing, the energy that maintains the body was being released.

The report shows the severity assessment went from urgent to critical at this point. The EKG monitor was attached and the "quick look" by Melody confirmed there was no heartbeat and that I was already in full arrest. Flat line. My heart had stopped and blood was no longer circulating to bring oxygen to the brain. I had died at approximately 1:35.

The thump from the paramedic's fist to save me was

unsuccessful, as were her repeated shouts for me to come back. Electric current—defibrillation—was then applied in three different charges, the final one stimulating my heart sufficiently to produce an electrical impulse and record a slow beat. After nearly four minutes, the life force was returning. A breath came, oxygen was given, full breathing resumed. I was back from the other side of death.

Most of us never think about having a heart attack, and that's good. But we should at least understand what it's all about so that we can be prepared if the time ever comes. With that in mind, I want to share information from a booklet called *Heart Attack* published by the American Heart Association.[1]

A heart attack can strike anyone. When it occurs, there is no time to delay. Most heart attack victims survive if they recognize the early warning signs of heart attack and get medical care at once.

When you suffer a heart attack, every minute counts. Don't wait. Get help immediately. Be sure you know these signs, because they may save your life.
- Uncomfortable pressure, fullness, squeezing or pain in the center of the chest lasting more than a few minutes.
- Pain may spread to the shoulders, neck or arms.
- Chest discomfort with lightheadedness, fainting, sweating, nausea or shortness of breath may also occur.

The early warnings of heart attack are a special "body language." They tell you that the blood supply to the heart is seriously reduced. A *coronary artery*, which supplies the heart with blood, has become narrowed or closed. As a result, part of the heart muscle isn't getting the blood and oxygen it needs and has begun to die. Doctors call this a *myocardial infarction*.

Coronary atherosclerosis causes heart attack. It's a slow process that can go on for years without causing any symptoms. Fatty deposits build up along the inner walls of the arteries to the heart. Much like lime deposits forming in a water pipe, atherosclerosis coats the inside of the artery channels and gradually narrows them. The fatty buildup reduces the flow of blood from the artery to an area of the heart muscle. When the blood flow stops due to a blockage—usually from a blood clot—a heart attack results.

The AHA booklet also says that "[t]he most feared outcome is sudden cardiac death (SCD). The most common heart rhythm in SCD is ventricular fibrillation. . . . If ventricular fibrillation isn't treated immediately, SCD will occur." That's what happened to me.

Carl, a tall, slender young man with dark hair and mustache, told John later: "When I saw her eyes roll back up, I knew she was gone, and most people don't come back after a sudden full arrest like this one."

He said that as soon as he and Melody saw the heartbeat activity on the monitor, he called Baptist Hospital in San Antonio for the Airlife helicopter. Estimated time of arrival: eight minutes. Then he called the EMS station in Boerne for another ambulance to bring the third paramedic and meet us at the main road leading into town.

John watched events unfold from what seemed like a distance.

"As strange as it may seem, I felt little or no emotion during the proceedings," he said. "There was a sense of detachment from the frantic activity that was going on before me, as though I was watching a 911 episode on television.

"Once Jan was on the stretcher and went into full cardiac arrest, I heard the words 'We've lost her.' Melody applied the 'precardial thump,' then turned to me and asked, 'What's her first name?' I told her and she began yelling, 'Jan, get back in here! Jan, get back in this body now!' Then came the electric paddles. Watching Jan's body recoil from the shocks, and seeing the flat line on the monitor still didn't seem to faze me. And while I knew well what was happening, I could not accept the idea that the woman I loved so dearly, so deeply, had actually died right there in front of me.

"And then, through some aperture in consciousness, I saw something that brought the reality home to me. At first I thought it was my imagination, but even after closing my eyes tightly and opening them again, the manifestation remained. Jan was slowly leaving her body, moving up above it—not as a ghostly apparition—but as a materialization in full form, complete with a flowing green gown. And then she *disappeared, and the monitor continued to reflect the full heart arrest."*

The next thing I remember is watching the scenario from somewhere above the action. As I observed, I was thinking, *This is not a dream. This is really happening to me. It is real. How strange. EMS. Heart attack. I'm dying. It's so easy. I'm just not in my body anymore, but I feel and think the same. This is going to be inconvenient for John; he doesn't know where everything is. And I didn't do the laundry.*

John continued:

"What I saw next—*after watching Jan leave her body—made me think that I was possibly in a state of shock and that another stretcher might be needed. I've hesitated in speaking of this, not only because of the credibility factor but because I'm just not in the habit of seeing EMS teams coming in from the other side of the veil to assist in a life-and-death situation. First I saw our dog, Maggi, who had died only weeks before, standing beside the stretcher. She disappeared in a split second, and five people suddenly materialized, obviously unseen by the paramedics. There were two women and three men, more ethereal than physical, and each one began to work on Jan. They didn't touch her body, but seemed to be massaging and fanning the energy around it.*

"One of the women was someone who had worked in my advertising agency in Houston in the early seventies.

When she died in 1975, she was only about thirty-five.
I also recognized the face of the other woman, but
couldn't put a name to it. The three men all had their
backs to me. When Jan started breathing again after being
clinically dead for several minutes (Melody's term
for Jan's condition), the five beings of light vanished
from my sight. It was then that I heard Carl call for a
backup ambulance and another paramedic to meet them
on the way to the helicopter.

"Melody handed me the EKG equipment to carry,
and they rushed Jan out of the house to the ambulance—
telling me to follow them to the high school soccer
field, where the helicopter would land."

Melody reported, "We departed the scene at 1:45,
and on the way established the IV and began adminis-
tering lidocaine [a drug used as a local anesthetic and
to control irregularity in the heartbeat]. We also called
Methodist Hospital in San Antonio to notify them that
she would be brought there by the Baptist Hospital
Airlife helicopter, and to report on her condition."

I later heard of something that happened at this particular juncture in the proceedings, and it touched me
deeply. When we reached the intersection of our country road and the main highway leading into town, the
second ambulance arrived with another paramedic—Pat
McClure—who jumped into our vehicle while the sheriff's cars blocked traffic.

Jack, who works in my office, arrived in the first car
coming from town that was stopped by the officers. Di-

rectly across from him in the southbound lane was Mike, a good friend of several years. While neither knew that I was in the ambulance, I felt that somehow their presence formed a passageway of light and love for me.

"As *the ambulance was leaving our driveway, I started my car," John recalls, "then remembered her purse and went back into the house to find it. Minutes later I was at the soccer field. No helicopter yet, but a crowd had quickly gathered—police and sheriff cars, a fire truck, two ambulances, people in small groups, and a number of private vehicles with curious onlookers. As I was running toward the ambulance, I was suddenly stopped by sheriff's deputies, and was held back even after I told them I was the patient's husband. She had to be dead, I thought, and they were trying to protect me. Finally Melody yelled at them to let me through, and when I reached the back of the ambulance, I could see that Jan's eyes were open, but it was obvious she didn't recognize me."*

Memories on the physical plane are pretty scanty here, but I do remember seeing John's face at the soccer field and thinking, "Don't drive fast." I thought I said it, but he says not. Knowing him, it probably wouldn't have made any difference anyway. I recall nothing of the ambulance ride into town, but do remember hearing the sound of the approaching helicopter. In fact somewhere in my mind I thought the helicopter was landing at our house. Unfortunately the entire helicopter trip to the hospital is also a blank.

According to the records, I was hooked up to machines for heart and pulse monitoring, given oxygen, and injected with more lidocaine. We have a report from Airlife Flight Communications to Kendall County EMS. Here's part of it: "During the 11 minute flight to San Antonio, Mrs. Price's vital signs, EKG, SaO_2, were continuously monitored. The patient complained of slight chest pain for which nitroglycerine was administered with some relief. The patient remained in a sinus rhythm throughout the flight. While en route, Methodist was called with a patient report, and an ETA."

As we approached the hospital, I heard the helicopter sound again and someone telling me that we were almost there and that a number of people would be meeting me and asking lots of questions. Then we landed, and I was surrounded by the medical team. We were moving fast, and all kinds of things were being attached to me. Someone was cutting my shirt with scissors. Someone else removed my rings, then clipped the end of the nail on my left index finger and put a funny little box on it. My finger felt strange and empty without my wedding rings. Everything seemed unreal. I was there, but somehow detached from all the activity, more as an observer. The people surrounding me were kind and pleasant. I can still recall some of their faces.

The EMS transmission from Boerne and the in-flight communications with the hospital provided sufficient time to call in a top heart specialist—Dr. Ricardo A.

Garza, a member of the American Board of Cardiovascular Diseases and, at the time, in practice with South Texas Cardiology Associates. He arrived as I entered the emergency room.

He later told John that he was quite surprised at my normal breathing and alertness, that this usually isn't the case with people who had experienced full cardiac arrests. He also indicated that the Boerne EMS team had obviously saved my life, and as Carl, the paramedic, said in a subsequent conversation, "The timing was critical, but it was a classic picture-perfect case of everything going right—precisely by the book." Again, the angels were watching over me.

Dr. Garza, young, handsome (I especially liked his eyes), and self-assured—yet with a warm and caring manner—quickly reviewed the corrective procedures available, including open-heart surgery. He said that a backup heart surgeon would be standing by if that was necessary. I listened to him and thought, *I don't need to do all that*, but felt no resistance to anything. He told me he would prefer to have my husband's permission as well as mine, but that he could not delay much longer. Then I saw John.

"Here he is now," I said, and heard Dr. Garza repeating all the things he had said to me. Then they took me to a large room that felt like a frozen-food locker. I don't remember much, but I'll never forget the extreme cold—and all those masked people looking down at me.

In this world of change naught which comes stays,
and naught which goes is lost.
—*Madame Swetchine (1782–1857),*
Russian mystic

2

My Husband Remembers

My near-death experience was not something I went through alone. Although John didn't accompany me on my journey, everything that happened on this side of the veil was mentally and emotionally recorded by him. So in many aspects it was a shared experience, and in this chapter, the words are his. He begins at the soccer field that Thursday afternoon in December. The paramedics had just placed me in the helicopter, and according to the Airlife records, the time was 2:11.

What follows is John's report, beginning at the soccer field, Thursday afternoon, December 30th:

"As the Airlife helicopter lifted off, I turned away from the gust of wind and flying leaves and found myself face-to-face with a burly deputy sheriff. Strong hands gripped my shoulders, and narrowed eyes behind the sunglasses carried a warning—yet this time the voice was gentle, and he spoke with a tenderness that almost brought tears to my eyes.

" 'You okay?' I nodded. 'All right, you take it easy now driving in to San Antonio. Your wife's in good hands, and she sure wouldn't want you to get all banged up driving too fast. No sense having both of you laid up in the hospital at the same time.'

"I agreed and thanked him for his concern, then headed for my car. As I started up, I noticed that his car was behind me, and he proceeded to follow me through town, then turned around when I pulled into a service station. Wouldn't you know, the gas tank was empty. We had driven to Austin the day before to do some shopping, and something told me to fill it back up when we returned. Should have listened. I quickly pumped in five dollars' worth, literally threw the bill at the attendant, and was finally on my way.

"I called the office when I reached Interstate 10 to give the staff a report, then settled in with seat belt fastened for the short drive. Thank God the highway patrol was watching for speeders on another road.

"It's about thirty-five miles from Boerne to San Antonio. Carl had said that Jan would be taken to Methodist Hospital, and had given me directions. I was glad she was going there, because the Heart Center at Methodist is rated as one of the finest cardiovascular diagnosis and treatment facilities around. I was feeling good about her receiving the best of care when, for some reason, my mind slipped into a down gear.

"Weaving in and out of traffic, I thought about having to make funeral arrangements, remembered that Jan wanted

to be cremated, then became very agitated because
my mother was fiercely opposed to cremation. Good
Lord, *I thought,* it's a no-win situation. Follow Jan's
wishes and I'm in trouble, but not to do so would
violate a trust. And how am I going to break the
news to our daughters that they've lost their
mother?

"Once on the morbid thought-track, it's tough to break
loose. I wondered if the helicopter had landed at the
hospital yet, and if I would get there in time. There
were so many things I wished I had said to her this morning.
And we should have made love last night instead of racking
our brains trying to decide where to go on a vacation
in January. Maybe if we had celebrated Christmas
on a Caribbean island, this wouldn't have happened.

"Fortunately a horn honking in displeasure at my cutting
in too close helped me to refocus, and as I took the
exit ramp off the freeway, my mind cleared. A feeling
of peace came over me, and I saw Jan's smiling face,
the large, dark, shimmering eyes, and I knew it
wasn't her time to go. I said aloud, 'You're going to
be okay, baby. We've got too much living to do for you
to leave now.' And I heard a 'Yes!' echo throughout
my being.

"Vividly seeing her beautiful face and form in my mind,
I laughed and thought deeply about this wonderful,
multifaceted woman I live with. She's highly intelligent
with few pretenses, is seldom moody, and loves life
with a passion. I thought about her playing with the
gleefulness of an uninhibited child, then turning around

*and exuding the earthiness of a woman who greatly
appreciates sensuous pleasures. My mind seemed to
be filled with her presence. I saw her moving gracefully
with quiet sophistication in every social situation, getting
things done with unthreatening authority when she
wears a business hat, and felt the glow of simply being
with her—sometimes without a word being exchanged
between us—just knowing the love we share in our oneness.
I've really never known anyone quite like Jan, and
right then all I wanted to do was hold her.*

"I pulled into a parking space near the emergency room
and ran to the door. Stepping inside, I heard someone
say, 'Are you Mr. Price?' I turned to see a large man
with a clerical collar approaching me.

" 'Yes,' I said.

"He held out his hand while identifying himself as the
hospital chaplain.

"The chaplain? Why would they send the chaplain
to meet me? Oh God, she must be gone, I thought,
and he's here to comfort me. All I could say in
that terrible moment of resignation was one word: 'Shit!'

" 'No, no . . . your wife is alive. I was sent by the
doctor to find you. Come, I'll take you to her.'

"I followed him down the hall and through the
double doors. There she was, along with a team of doctors
and nurses. They looked up as I entered, and motioned
me to hurry. What I remember most at this point
is looking into Jan's eyes and knowing again with all
my heart that she was going to make it. Somewhere in
the background I could hear a doctor's voice explaining

*the options to me, the risks involved, and the
percentage of people who survived each procedure.
Then a nurse asked me to quickly sign the release forms
so that they could get started.*

"I turned to the nurse and asked, 'Is he any good?'

*" 'The best,' she said. I don't know what I would
have done if she had said otherwise. 'Go on up to the
fifth-floor waiting room,' she added, 'and the doctor will
meet you there as soon as he has something to tell
you.' Then she handed me Jan's wedding rings. The
symbolism of that action bothered me for a moment.*

*"Once in the dimly lit waiting room—I was the only
one there—all I could do was pray. It wasn't the
usual prayer of asking God to save a loved one but
rather to express my thankfulness to the Spirit of God
in Jan—and within each doctor and nurse—for the splendid
healing that I knew was taking place at that very
moment. I praised the lifeforce for its renewing,
perfecting action, and acknowledged that there was only
vital livingness and harmonious expression in every
atom and cell of her body.*

*"Then I looked up to see someone enter the room.
It was Walter Starcke, a dear friend and owner of
the Guadalupe River Ranch, where we had our offices
at the time. He said, 'I didn't come for Jan—she's going
to be all right—I came for you.' And he sat beside me
and we meditated together and talked until the doctor
came in a couple of hours later.*

*"The doctor told us that he had used a catheter to
inject dye into Jan's heart. This procedure was necessary*

to make pictures of the heart and arteries to determine the cause of the arrest and the damage done. He reported that the blocked coronary artery was on the left side and that he had felt that it should be treated with angioplasty and had done so.

"Angioplasty is a surgical technique in which a tiny balloon at the end of a long, fine tube is inserted into a vein in the groin, pushed up into the affected artery, inflated to clear the blockages and improve the blood flow, and then removed. The doctor said Jan would be taken into intensive care shortly and that I could visit her, but that it would be several hours before he could tell us the extent of the heart damage and give a complete prognosis.

"With Jan seemingly out of the woods at this point, Walter gave me a big hug and said good-bye, and I went up to the ICU waiting room. What a difference. This one was jammed full with men, women, and children—sleeping, praying, talking, reading, eating, watching television—not a seat available. So I paced and counted the gleaming white squares of tile in the hall until I got the word that I could go in to the unit. It was six-thirty that evening.

"Since she was still fairly sedated, I kissed her and stayed only a few minutes, telling the nurse that I was going to the telephone to make some necessary calls and that I'd be back in half an hour. Our youngest daughter, Leslie, lives in France, and with the seven-hour time difference I decided to wait until about eleven o'clock our time to call her. Susan, our oldest, wasn't

*at home in Austin, so I called my mother to report what
had happened. Still no answer at Susan's on my second
call to her. Jan's mother was in a nursing home, and
I thought it best to delay speaking to her until I could
do it in person.*

"When I returned to the ICU, I saw the attendants
*hurriedly pushing Jan's bed toward the elevator. Seeing
me start to run toward them, one of the attendants said
they were on their way to the operating room to
dissolve a clot that had formed in an artery and for
me to go back to the waiting room. While my mind told
me that Jan was out of danger and on the road to recovery,
I'll have to admit that my emotions were still a bit
raw and tender. I felt so tired, so helpless, and my
aversion to waiting rooms was now moving into the hate
category—but my spirits were quickly lifted by the sight
of Melody and Carl, the EMS paramedics from
Boerne, who were getting off the elevator. They had
come to check on Jan, and I was visibly moved by their
kindness and concern.*

"An hour and a half later I was sitting beside Jan's
*bed in intensive care, holding her hand and smiling and
trying to think of something humorous to say—but
a comedian I'm not in situations like this. All I could
do was tell her how much I loved her and how much
she meant to me. After a few minutes of listening to
my mutterings, I could tell that she was more
concerned about me than she was about herself.*

" 'Have you eaten?' she asked. When I said no, she
insisted that I go home, eat something, and go to bed.

Sensing my reluctance, she asked, 'Have you called the girls?' I told her I had tried to call Susan, but there was no answer. I said I would go home and try her again, and then call Leslie in France. I kissed her good-bye and headed for the elevator.

"A nurse caught up with me before I reached it and asked for our home telephone number. When I asked why, she said, 'Just in case we need to reach you during the night.' My mind immediately went back to May 1954, when the hospital called in the middle of the night to tell me that our baby boy had died. That memory came up for replay several times on the drive home.

"I arrived at the house about ten-thirty and called Susan in Austin. She was still up, and when she answered, I said, "Susie, before I say anything else, I want you to know that everything is okay, so don't get scared.'

" 'Dad, what happened?'

"I told her the whole story, beginning with her mother not feeling well that morning. She listened quietly, asked a few questions, then said that she would pack a bag and leave right away. It's a one-and-a-half-hour drive to Boerne, so I suggested that she get some sleep and come over early the next morning. She agreed, saying that she would be at the house by seven.

"At eleven that night I called Leslie in Nice. I began with the 'everything is okay' line, then said, 'Mother had a heart attack.'

"And she said, 'Your mother, or my mother?'

" 'Your mother.'

" 'Oh, Daddy!'

" 'Now, don't cry, because if you do, I'm going to fall apart, so hang in there.' I gave her all the details, then five hours later, at four o'clock in the morning our time—while I was sitting straight up in bed wondering if the telephone was going to ring—Leslie called the hospital from France and asked for a full report from the intensive care nurse. Guess she wanted to make sure that I wasn't holding anything back. I was told about this when Susan and I arrived at the hospital early the next morning.

"As we walked into the ICU, we heard Jan laughing and exclaiming to one of the nurses, 'Hey, I feel so good, I could go home!'

"Those were the most beautiful words I'd ever heard. I smiled at Susan. 'Darlin', that's your mother talking . . . and if I know her, they're not going to be able to keep her here very long.'

"When the doctor came in later that morning, he told Susan and me that Jan had 'amazing recuperative powers,' which he attributed to her 'excellent health.' I remember Susan saying, 'If she's so healthy, why did she have a heart attack?'

" 'It was more of a malfunction than an illness,' he said. 'She has a very positive body.'

"After hearing the doctor's report, I left Susan with Jan and went up to the coffee shop on the top floor of the hospital, which opens out to the roof. Sitting there on a bench in the crisp, cool air, I expressed my gratitude to God, the angels, and everyone who had said a prayer on her behalf. And then I thought about life . . . and I thought about death.

"The French author Madame de Staël (1766–1817) wrote, 'We understand death for the first time when he puts his hand upon one whom we love.' Jan and I had not talked much about death over the years. It was something that we knew we both would face, but way down the road in another time. Then when I saw her die, my first thought was one that she would later put into words: 'It's so easy.'

"And that's where my new understanding of death focused initially: on the ease of it, how it can happen suddenly, and that you don't have to be sick to die. The great simplicity of dying can allay many fears about the process. I know it did for me, but because there is a permanent ending, it also makes you more aware of the inevitability of change in life.

"Our good friend Robert Brumet wrote a book called Finding YourSelf in Transition, in which he said,

Everything in this phenomenal world has at least one thing in common; it all had a beginning, and it all will come to an end. . . . Our physical body had a beginning, and it will have an end. Each beginning is a type of birth, each ending a type of death.

We in the Western world are generally not comfortable with death in any form. We tend to acknowledge and celebrate beginnings and to deny and lament end-

ings. We rejoice at a birth yet often see death as a trag-
edy.

To live fully is to realize that death—any type of
death—is but a harbinger of new life.[1]

"*F*ortunately Jan came back, postponing the inevitable,
so our 'new life' together would be a continuation of
our blessed oneness on this plane—until that moment
when we would be temporarily separated. Yes, I
thought, there would be a time when one of us would
go out ahead of the other. Suddenly, sitting there on the
roof of the hospital that morning, her death-and-return
experience became a loud wake-up call for me: Don't
take her for granted; don't waste time, it's too precious;
live more, love more, laugh more.

"Yes! Death does force you to think more about
life—and a near-death episode is like another chance
at life. It makes you focus on what a relationship is all
about, the purpose of the bonding, the real meaning of
love, and not missing the opportunity to truly live
every moment while still in the physical body. Brumet
was right. Any type of death, and perhaps even more
so with near-death, is a harbinger of new life.

"We were embarking on a new beginning. Death's
hand had touched Jan, but it wasn't her time. There
was just too much living still to do on this plane."

> Guilt is the source of sorrow, the avenging fiend,
> that follows us behind with whips and stings.
> —Nicholas Rowe (1674–1718),
> English poet

3

Where It All Began

I had absolutely no fear—not during the heart attack, nor during the death experience, nor afterward. The heart attack was simply increasing discomfort—not frightening, just a growing realization that something was wrong with my body. And though the pain and pressure intensified, I still didn't become apprehensive; I just kept thinking how inconvenient this was. Even when we called EMS, I don't think I really understood the seriousness of my situation.

I remember being surprised as I observed the full heart arrest taking place. I suppose we never really think of ourselves as dying, but obviously I had died because I wasn't in my body anymore.

Then suddenly I felt something on both sides of me, not as we might describe a physical touch, but more as a *feeling*, a sensation of a presence—of entities, more than one. I could see their light as forms of energy, and I realized that they were angelic beings—

loving, pure, holy, helpful. They were assisting me, and I felt an upward movement. Then everything was blue.

I saw and felt the most beautiful blue—neither light nor dark blue, but luminous blue. Floating in this ocean of light-filled blue, I was serene, tranquil, free, and could have happily stayed there forever.

The Wise Ones have said that blue is the color of God, the universal spiritual color, and I know that I have never felt such peace—a peace beyond calm, beyond words. It is indescribable ecstasy, quiet joy, liquid love; a feeling of incredible ease, the pure pleasure of being with no concern for doing—being one with all that is, suspended and supported in a sea of love. Merging with the energy of all that is came the feeling of completeness—and an utter contentment in being complete—a moving into myself and knowing the fullness of me. Then came the golden light—gold, the color of our individual spiritual nature.

Suspended in the ocean of blue, golden streams of light—like stardust—began to pour through me. The light felt so good. If I harbored any lingering heaviness from my life on earth, I knew it was being taken away. And as the radiation continued, I realized there was no longer any sense of gravity, no pulls from the past, only a feeling of being ethereal, gossamer in lightness. Then, like a sweet elixir, the shining rays infusing me washed to the surface a lifetime of memories, beginning with my birth.

It was ten minutes before midnight on a warm June night when I entered the body, which was finally being released from my mother. And there in the glaring light stood a lot of angry people. I figured that I must have done something wrong, since they were so upset.

They thought the woman who was my mother might die. She had been trying to have this baby for several days before they decided to remove it surgically. Since that was the body I was now inhabiting, I guessed it would be my fault if she died. That must be why everyone seemed to be mad at me. Lord, what a way to start a life. I just got here and am already guilty of wrongdoing.

Someone took me down the hall to another room and left me by myself. To tell the truth, I was relieved to get out of the operating room. The brightness was blinding, and the strange sounds seemed blaring and raucous. Being handled was not unpleasant, though it was unfamiliar, but brisk movement was disconcerting. The tiny body was limiting and uncontrollable, unable to do anything for itself, and could not communicate feelings and needs except by a wailing sound. There was no choice but to continue in this confined state, for life had begun a new journey.

Later I would learn that the angry people were family members and friends, all frustrated with the old doctor who had let things go on much too long. They were all jammed into the little operating room of the small hospital where I began this life, and they weren't mad at me. I hadn't done anything wrong, but the die was cast.

The impression had been made on my mind and emotions, and a guilt pattern was set that I would carry until I died.

Now the picture seems to fast-forward and I'm a little girl. I'm very pretty, and Mother and Daddy look so young. As an only child, adored by my parents, childhood is a happy time. There I am in my bunny fur coat, hat, and muff, and am now onstage being crowned the winner of the Shirley Temple contest.

But the tap dance in Mother's Sunday-school class at the Baptist church doesn't seem to go over very well. And I see me being very frightened when I was put in the closet for doing or saying something that wasn't approved of.

Now a hospital scene when surgery was needed on my ears—mastoid, they called it. Every day people would come to my room and wrap me up in a sheet so that I couldn't move. It terrified me and I would beg and plead for them not to do it. Mother and Daddy didn't stop them no matter how I cried. They just stood and watched. I felt helpless, overpowered, and no one would help me, not even those I trusted most. Then I saw their faces, so young and frightened, and I could tell that they loved me so much. It was not their fault, but at three years old I didn't know that.

Birthday parties, picnics, trips on the train, wonderful experiences with family and friends. Still, subtle misconceptions that I had done something wrong were drawn to that early guilt pattern like a magnet. I felt that if I did or said what I really wanted to do or say, I would get in trouble. Part of me had to stay in the closet or else I would do something wrong.

School days were great, except that time in first grade when the teacher put a sign on me that said BABY. I had been talking in class. Humiliating! In second grade I was sent out of rhythm band for the same offense. I hid in the hall until school was out because I was so embarrassed.

Growing up, lots of friends, overnights, always pets, inspiring teachers, discovering the wonder of books. Boyfriends, dances, high school—there I am in my majorette costume.

When I was fifteen, Daddy died. He was only forty-five when a massive heart attack took him instantly. A few months before, two of my friends' fathers had died, and I had thought a lot about it, wondering what it would be like. Was that what caused Daddy's death—was it my fault? Mother said I let her down because I wasn't there for her when it happened. I was out with some friends, and she couldn't locate me for quite some time. It felt funny not to have Daddy there, and Mother became increasingly dependent on me. She wanted me to take care of her, and I really didn't want to. More guilt.

Graduation. What do I do now? Everyone is going to college, so I guess I will too. Off I go. It feels kind of strange not to be in a place where everyone knows me. I've never experienced this before, and feel a bit uncomfortable at first. Activities begin, I get involved, it's fun.

Then John, seeing him across the room at that December party and knowing instantly that we would always be together. Our wedding, living in Germany our first year of marriage, for he's in the Air Force. A magical time.

Our little boy died. He only lived one day. If I had realized the extent of the problem in my pregnancy, maybe he would have been all right. Two daughters, Susan, then Leslie. Precious children, a pure delight. As they grow up and encounter problems in their lives, I'm sure it's my fault. I feel responsible. I should have been a better mother.

I see a recent entry in my journal, written the day after our beloved dog died: "Sadness. Guilt. I should have done more for her, helped her, spent more time with her, taken better care of her, known how much she was hurting. Could I ever do enough? Could I ever think I did enough? I don't like the way 'it' works. Pain and suffering and death are not right—nor grief. I want it to be different. Yesterday I felt guilty for feeling relief, for not grieving enough. Guilt is so ugly. I miss her. A lot. I see her everywhere, and yet she isn't here. Sometimes I hear her woof, but it is not so. My darling John is hurting so. I need to help him. I need help for me! This, too, will pass."

What I saw on that incredibly fast memory train was a subconscious pattern of guilt and how it had developed over time. Consciously I wasn't aware of the depth of the pain, for my life has been a wonderful adventure. Happiness has been my companion. But guilt demands punishment, the death penalty in my case—which is fine because with the guilt eliminated, I am now free to live life joyously.

Regarding guilt and punishment, Kenneth Wapnick, clinical psychologist, says that guilt

> is an all-pervasive sense of alienation, isolation and helplessness that remains with us from the moment of birth to our death.
>
> Once we feel guilty, it is equally impossible not to feel deserving of punishment for what we have done wrong, and to fear the form this punishment will take. . . . The belief in our guilt unconsciously leads us to expect reprisal, and so we walk this earth in constant fear, believing that tragedy or catastrophe stalks our every step.[1]

And of course we take those fears with us when we journey to the other side—only to find that there's no such thing as unforgiveness. I realized this on my trip, and again when I received a little book from a friend entitled *Intra Muros* (Into Heaven) after I returned from the hospital.[2] It was written in the 1800s by Rebecca Ruter Springer about her near-death experience. Rebecca, born in Indianapolis in 1832, was the daughter of a Methodist Episcopal minister. Here are some excerpts from a chapter on the meaning of forgiveness in heaven:

> Many precious hours of intercourse were spent in my dear father's home, and sometimes on rare occasions I was permitted to accompany him to his field of la-

bor and assist him in instructing those lately come into the new life with little or no preparation for its duties and responsibilities. On one occasion he said to me:

"I have the most difficult problem to deal with I have ever yet met in this work. It is how to enlighten and help a man who suddenly plunged from an apparently honorable life into the very depths of crime. I have never been able to get him to accompany me to the river, where these earthly cobwebs would be swept from his poor brain; his excuse being always that God's mercy is so great in allowing him inside heaven's gates at all, that he is content to remain always in the lowest scale of enjoyment and life.

"He was led astray by infatuation for a strange woman, and killed his aged mother in order to secure her jewels. He was executed for the crime, of which in the end he sincerely repented, but he left life with all the horror of the deed clinging to his soul."

"Has he seen his mother since coming here? Does she know of his arrival?"

"No . . ."

"May I bring her?"

"Yes, bring her."

I was soon on my way. I laid the facts gently before her . . . in an instant she said, "My poor boy. Certainly I will go with you at once."

We found the young man seated beneath one of the flower-laden trees, gently perusing a book that my father had left with him. After a time he glanced up and saw his mother standing near him. A startled look came into his face, and he rose to his feet. She extended her arms toward him ... "John, my dear boy, come home to me—I need you!"

With a low cry he knelt at her feet and clasped her knees, sobbing, "Mother! Mother!"

She stooped and put her tender arms around him; she drew his head gently to her breast and showered kisses on his bowed head.

Beyond the curtain, there is nothing to forgive. There is only unconditional love.

Because the collective human consciousness believes in sorrow and suffering, guilt trips were a part of my life, too, along with the appropriate sentences of punishment. If I had known then what I know now, I would have let my mind be healed of all imaginary shortcomings, thus moving my physical body out of harm's way. Simply put, the body does not have the power by itself to become ill or to malfunction; the cause always originates on some level of consciousness.

My journal writings were filled with hints of what was going on in the subconscious realm, and my dreams were very vivid in their warnings. For example, a month prior to the journal entry noted earlier, I recorded a dream. I wrote, "Disturbing dream last night. Plumbing stopped up in house, water won't drain. Thick, muddy residue piling up everywhere—even in other towns. Roto-Rooter can't possibly clear it all. Then I go in a room, and when I start to leave, a long snake is hanging on a hook on the inside of the door.

I get up on a table to get away and there are snakes hanging from the ceiling. They start to be lowered, and I'm yelling, 'No!' "

This was a warning that I apparently did not heed. Looking at the symbols in retrospect, I can see that "plumbing" refers to the system of arteries, and "water that won't drain" to blood that can't flow through the obstructions that are building up. Roto-Rooter (angioplasty?) can't clear it all—there must also be a healing in consciousness. Snakes are often reminders of what we may consider the unredeemed part of our nature—our so-called "sins"—and guilt is definitely a transgression of the law of life. (Angioplasty surgery is also a "snakelike" technique in which the tube with the tiny balloon moves up through the arteries.)

As the golden light continued to flow, I knew that there was a purpose in the radiation. Old error patterns based mostly on guilt were being dissolved. I was going back into the body without them, for it wasn't time for me to leave permanently. That was one of the good things about dying. The emotional system was cleaned, and all the false guilt was washed away. The little girl could come out of the closet. She had never done anything wrong.

The last thing I had written in my journal before the heart attack flashed into my mind. One word. *Transformation*. Then the journey into the Beyond continued.

Life is a flower of which love is the honey.
—*Victor Hugo (1802–1885),*
French author

4

The Love Connection

As the density changed, becoming lighter and finer, I felt that I was being lifted to another level of awareness—and then I found myself in surroundings that appeared to be more substantial—Maggi was there. My beautiful dog, my beloved springer, came to me. She had died less than a month before, and John and I still ached from her absence.

I felt her presence, her love, and she appeared to me as she had when she was in physical form—only younger, more vital. She said, "You know that Daddy can't handle both of us being gone right now."

"Yes, I'm going back," I replied. "Will you come soon?"

"When it is time, we will know. Now I will show you wondrous things. Let's explore together."

If you are having difficulty accepting the idea that my first encounter on the other side was with a dog, you aren't the only one. While John thought it perfectly natural, one of our daughters became a little upset when I told her about it. I think she would have preferred that her mother be greeted by Jesus, an angel, or at least by a family member. I did meet a Master Teacher—I'll get to that later—but Maggi came first. After all, she had been close "family" for many years, and whoever is responsible for setting up the Welcome Wagon over there certainly knew what a delightful experience it would be for me to be greeted by her.

But I did understand our daughter's reaction. If Mother was going to have the opportunity of visiting beyond the veil, the least she could do was make it awe-inspiring with some dramatic religious overtones. Fact of the matter is there is nothing particularly "religious" about the other side. *Spiritual*, yes, but nothing "characterized by adherence to religion or a religion"— to use Webster's definition of the term. As Harold Richter Stark, M.D., said after his near-death experience and tour of the other side, "One does not go around in an ecstasy of religious fervor, but it is a place of ordered activity."[1]

What I came to realize is that there is a love connection between the two worlds—a stream of energy that forms a heart bond between two souls that is the strongest at the time of transition. Love comes out to greet you, wearing the form that will be most meaningful to you at the time. In my case it was our precious dog, and yes, dogs have souls—Plato knew it and so did Saint Augustine, along with most other true saints and sages.

And yes, they can communicate audibly in our language in that other world. They have done so in the physical realm, too, as evidenced in certain passages of the Bible.

Later at home after my recovery, I discovered in Joseph Campbell's writings that "Animals are our equals at least, and sometimes our superiors. The animal has powers that the human doesn't have. The shaman, for instance, will often have an animal familiar, that is to say, the spirit of some animal species that will be his support and his teacher."[2]

I also found that animals were held in veneration by all races of antiquity, and ancient wisdom texts tell us that "The dog, because of its faithfulness, denotes the relationship which should exist between disciple and master or between the initiate and his God. The dog's ability to sense and follow unseen persons for miles symbolizes the transcendental power by which the philosopher follows the thread of truth through the labyrinth of earthly error. The dog is also the symbol of Mercury."[3] (Mercury was the messenger of the gods in Roman mythology.)

Valerie Moolman, author of *The Meaning of Your Dreams*, has written that "People who are particularly fond of dogs tend to regard them, unconsciously, as human beings, and to identify very closely with them."[4] This is especially true in what we call the nonphysical world, where all relationships are on a higher frequency. Even though we take our consciousness with us (we don't instantly become totally enlightened), we find that our thoughts and feelings are more in tune with the spiritual reality of all that is. And what is "spiritual"? To me it is the true inner essence of everything—the rock, the tree, the animal, the person. It is the spirit, the unique field of energy within each mineral, plant, animal, and human.

So Maggi and I were interacting on a finer wavelength, and although we had dropped our physical vehicles, our bodies were made visible to the senses through an image in the mind projected as form—and she was as real to see and touch as she was when I'd held her in my arms in the physical world.

One of my favorite authors, Ken Carey, has written about our spiritual friends—the "us" in the oneness of all life. In his book, *Flat Rock Journal*, he says,

Before and after this terrestrial biology, we are spirits, you and I. Longing for structures that would last for more than a moment, for more than an hour or a day, we came here to experience this warm and fertile world, to play upon its surface, to partake of it through forms of living clay. Some of us touch the earth through human forms, some through the forms of the owls and whippoorwills who fly these moonlit skies. Some of us swim as salmon in her streams or leap as dolphins in her seas. Some of us wear the fur of the four-footed and sniff the shifting of the ageless winds. And some of us, some of us express ourselves in the stately dances of these trees. I recognize them in the moon's soft light, these friends, old friends from before.[5]

My friend Maggi and I walked side by side as we had so many times in that other place of being. Without any effort we moved through a realm of ecstatic color. The pulsating, indescribable colors were fluid—energy waiting to be formed. Maggi showed me how to shape forms out of energy by pressing with my mind. If you want the form to hold, you press firmly. This is a highly mental plane, and form is created with no bodily effort. An image of that which you wish to create is held in mind, and through intense focus is brought into expression. You can lock it in, or release it.

This was so new to me then, but later I found that it was pretty much old hat to near-death experiencers. As Michael Talbot describes it in his book, *The Holographic Universe*, "When the mind is in the 'higher' frequencies of the near-death dimension, it continues to do what it does best, translate those frequencies into a world of appearances."[6] I'll talk more about this later.

Talbot also discusses the work of the Swedish mystic Emanuel Swedenborg (1688–1772), who was a "skilled out-of-body visitor to the land of the dead." He says that Swedenborg "believed that, despite its ghostlike and ephemeral qualities, heaven is actually a more fundamental level of reality than our own physical world . . . that the afterlife realm and physical reality are different in degree but not in kind, and that the material world is just a frozen version of the thought-built reality of heaven."[7]

I didn't experience "heaven" as ghostlike, but I do agree that the physical and nonphysical worlds have a distinct similarity, with the latter actually *feeling* more real. At least I felt a higher level of reality about myself while on that beautiful plane.

Regarding the colors, the wisdom teachings of the Tibetan master Djwhal Khul tell us that "Colours as manifested on the physical plane show as their crudest and harshest . . . as the finer matter of the other planes is contacted, the beauty, the softness and the exquisite quality of the different hues, grow . . . the beauty transcends all conception."[8]

Maggi and I played in the color field, stepping into various hues and feeling their particular vibration. The matchless quality of the colors fascinated me because I hadn't seen anything like them before, and cannot to this day find words to describe the beauty of the shades and hues. It's been said that "In addition to the colors of the spectrum there are a vast number of vibratory color waves, some too low and others too high to be registered by the human optical apparatus."[9]

While I didn't have a mirror on the other side, I recognized that I had a body and I experienced that I was looking through my eyes to see it, but what I was really observing through was my mind. Thus without the physical "optical apparatus," my awareness was expanded well beyond the seven fundamental color tones.

Each wave of color seemed to have a frequency of its own, giving off a particular sound that I interpreted as a beautiful chord of music—and dancing from color to color was like playing some cosmic musical instrument in the heavenly symphony. It was fun, and Maggi seemed to enjoy it too.

We've heard the expression "music of the spheres." I wasn't sure what that meant until my visit to the other side. There I heard the music divine, sometimes sounding like chants of angels, playing in the background. Later, when I told John about it, he remembered that the phrase was attributed to Pythagoras, who was born in 600 B.C. and considered the world's "first philosopher." He found the following reference in a book in our library:

> The Pythagoreans believed that everything which existed had a voice and that all creatures were eternally singing the praise of the Creator. Man fails to hear these divine melodies because his soul is enmeshed in the illusion of material existence. When he liberates himself from the bondage of the lower world with its sense limitations, *the music of the spheres* will again be audible as it was in the Golden Age. Harmony recognizes harmony, and when the human soul regains its true estate it will not only hear the celestial choir but also join with it in an everlasting anthem of praise to that Eternal *Good* controlling the infinite number of parts and conditions of Being.[10]

Moving on, we entered a lovely green meadow filled with flowers. Here we were walking with more of a sense of the movement of our bodies. This place reminded me of a vision I had experienced several years ago in which I picked a flower and held it in my hand, but it was also exactly where it was before. Wondering what would happen here, I reached for a blossom, and as I took it in my hand, another one appeared in its place. How wonderful! The beauty can't be marred. Nothing is lost. There is ever more of the substance that stands behind each expression, just waiting to flow into its perfect pattern of being.

Maggi wanted to show me where she lived, which she said was patterned by much of what she remembered of the homes where she had lived with us. She had held the images in her mind, pressed, and created a place of residence. As she spoke of her home, we arrived there, which didn't seem strange at all at the time. Later I realized that it was a rather bizarre experience—not only the instantaneous "being there" in the space of a thought but also the idea that our dog actually had a beautiful home on the other side. Again John later helped me to understand this when he said that Emanuel Swedenborg, a frequent visitor to the heavenly realm, wrote that animals do indeed have abodes in the spiritual world, pointing out that they "have such knowledge, for it is implanted in them to know of themselves their homes and dwelling places, as is evident from abundant observation."[11]

As I stood in Maggi's dwelling place, I felt great joy. There was a fire in the fireplace, giving the room a warm, friendly glow. A wall of books—of course! Beautiful paintings and oriental rugs. One whole side of the room was glass and you could look out on a vista of rolling hills, bubbling streams, and many trees.

We sat comfortably on one of the soft, velvety love

seats, content just to be together. I stroked her beautiful head and she laid her paws across my legs. To touch again was so precious, for there was so much love between us. Without spoken words we shared memories and deep feelings. Much communication over here was silent, although sound was sometimes used simply because it was so pleasant. My heart overflowed with gratitude for the opportunity to have this reunion—and see my loved one so joyously, vibrantly alive in what can truly be called paradise. Reluctantly we left Mag's lovely home, for I felt an inner prodding to move on.

Next we went to a place she called the lookout. It appeared to be only an overhang on a high cliff, but the view was intensely magnified. I could look into the world I had left behind as though peering into a monitor, if I chose to do so. No one spent a lot of time here, Maggi said, but some occasionally stopped by to check on what was going on in the earthly realm. I decided not to; I wanted to keep moving on in this world of exquisite bliss.

It is strange but true; for truth is always strange,
stranger than fiction.
—*Lord Byron (1788–1824),*
English poet

5

Perceptions
of Reality

Ralph Waldo Emerson said that we are what we
think about all day long. What this means is that
our thoughts and feelings set up a vibration in the energy field around us. As the particular *trend* of thought
continues, it impresses the energy and forms a pattern,
which begins to externalize itself as conditions, situations, and experiences in our lives. We literally create
our personal worlds through our belief system, and
that's why *consciousness* is said to be a self-fulfilling
prophecy. We always become what we think about.

That is particularly true in the higher realms. Structure and environment continue to be brought into
expression as a reflection of consciousness—as mind-
energy coming into form and experience—but the manifestation is so much faster. Time is different—not
limiting—because we are not conscious of it. Therefore
a person's belief system begins immediately to create a
complementary world and will continue to "outpicture"

such a world until consciousness changes and reality is revealed.

Time's measurement on the physical plane is based on the vibration rate of cesium atoms, which was approved by international agreement in 1964.

On the other side, time is simply the sequence of activity recorded in consciousness. And since our awareness is on a higher frequency in that world, progression (what we see happening) is greatly accelerated. In some situations it would seem to be at the speed of light.

In *Return from Tomorrow* George G. Ritchie, M.D., writes about his life review during a near-death experience: "There were other scenes, hundreds, thousands, all illuminated by that searing Light, in an existence where time seemed to have ceased. It would have taken weeks of ordinary time even to glance at so many events, and yet I had no sense of minutes passing."[1]

The specified lengths of time that we on earth call seconds, minutes, hours, days, and so forth do not apply over there. The Bible's definition of God's time (the plane of heaven) is that one thousand years equals one day—a remarkable extension of third-dimensional time. I was out of my body for close to four minutes. If we agree with the Bible equation, that would be about three years on the higher plane. That seems like an awfully long time for my particular experience; maybe I just didn't adjust to "heavenly time" the way others have. For example, in *Intra Muros* Rebecca Ruter

Springer says, "Days lengthened into weeks, and weeks into months, and these in turn crept into years, and the duties and joys of heaven grew clearer and dearer with each passing hour."[2]

It could be that the duration of my visit didn't register in consciousness because it was already determined that I would remain on the other side only until the high-energy cleansing process was completed. This would mean that on some level of consciousness I still had a strong attachment to my physical body, which would throw my cosmic clock out of kilter.

I also want to add something more about "outpicturing"—the idea that everything is a reflection of consciousness. In John's book *The Planetary Commission* he says that what we see in our world

are *ideas* in consciousness expressed on the third-dimensional plane. They are *your* images, and each image is nothing more nor less than your beliefs projected into materiality.

Everything comes to you or is repelled from you based on the vibration of your energy field, and the vibration is established by your beliefs and convictions. Accordingly, you can see that nothing is out of place or out of order in your life. Everything is perfect based on your consciousness and the outworking of the law. Your world is a mirror of your thoughts, feelings, concepts— all pressed out in material form and experience.

You simply cannot run away from your world because

you can't run away from yourself. You can't even escape by destroying your body, because you take your consciousness with you.[3]

Dr. Ritchie, quoted earlier, also writes about the immediate "outpicturing" of consciousness beyond the veil. He says, "Whatever anyone thought, however fleetingly or unwillingly, was instantly apparent to all around him, more completely than words could have expressed it, faster than sound waves could have carried it."[4]

Yes, we do take our consciousness with us when we die, and until it changes, we will continue to see a mirror of what we believe. Perhaps this is where the concept of heaven and hell originally began, because on the other side of death, our mind-sets are revealed to us in no uncertain terms. A higher, finer consciousness sees the good, while those mired in their lower nature will temporarily project a rather coarse type of existence. The average human being may experience a little of both until consciousness stabilizes in the clear light.

Since my visit I am more convinced than ever before that our time on earth must be devoted to attaining a higher consciousness—a deeper *spiritual* awareness. And not just to have healthier bodies and more material possessions. Those are the added things that come into our lives when we seek an understanding of the Reality of our Being—the Spirit of God within. And when we realize that Presence, and understand that *It* is who and what we are, then our lives become an adventure in love, joy, and peace, and the adventure continues when we cross over, in even fuller measure.

Let's move on now to my next adventure in the non-physical world.

Sensing the questions forming in my mind, Maggi informed me that we would go where all the answers are. Quickly (as I'd discovered is the way on this plane of existence) we approached a structure of supernal beauty. It was vast, of the purest white, and somewhat Grecian in architecture. Paths led into the structure from all directions, and I observed many people coming and going.

Both men and women wore soft, loose, mostly white flowing clothing, and I noticed that no one was really young or old—sort of a "middle" age. I figured that they looked exactly as they should for their optimal expression. Though we passed some of these people on our way, I really didn't want to stop and talk; and because I was so intent on where we were going—to where "the answers are"—no one intruded. It was as though they sensed that I was not yet ready for conversation.

Over the archway through which we entered the structure, I saw the words TEMPLE OF KNOWLEDGE and felt a gentle power drawing me into itself. There were pillars of varying heights, becoming higher and higher toward the center. Aware of the light and openness, I noticed there was no roof on the building. The outer perimeter reminded me of a veranda, and I saw small groups of people engaged in discussion.

I passed one lively group, and when I overheard the

conversation, I realized it was a gathering of writers sharing ideas. I wasn't surprised that I was drawn to this particular group, as it reminded me of the many exhilarating discussions that John and I have had over the years. I heard one woman say, "This is what I've been working on"—and with great animation she described her current writing project. Others in the group seemed to catch her excitement, and each, in his or her turn, began to offer ideas on how to enhance the subject.

Listening closely, I learned that the information shared in these groups was somehow "broadcast" into the denser plane of earth as seed ideas to be picked up by interested parties. This explained why writers in different parts of the world sometimes get the same idea for a book. This principle would also apply to the creation of inventions, scientific discoveries, new understanding of the great philosophies, and other advances. Those who have a strong interest in any particular discipline continue to expand their comprehension of the subject, though out of the physical body, thus doing a service for those incarnate.

From here I looked out upon the beautiful gardens—flowers, fruits, and plants of many varieties arranged in exquisite patterns. Here and there someone was tending them, and I felt a surge of happiness for the many I know—such as John's mother and her husband—who find such pleasure in growing things. It seems that nothing that brings real satisfaction is left behind.

Turning back to the interior of the temple, I saw that creative activities were taking place in different areas.

There were a number of individuals sitting at easels painting, and I saw one man playing a flutelike instrument that emitted the sweetest of sounds. Farther on, dancers moved with ethereal grace, performing with a lightness impossible to the physical human form. As I watched in utter delight, I became aware that the musical background for this visual feast came from what I would call a celestial choir—an orchestra of voices creating "heavenly" music for the dance. This "music of the spheres" was indeed singing the praises of the Creator.

What I was seeing certainly indicated that creative expression was given high priority here. In another area both groups and individuals were engaged in various art forms, some that we would call sports. There was no competition, simply joyful participation in activities that brought fulfillment.

The sound of laughter drew my attention back to the outside. Children were playing on a grassy expanse leading to a small pond. Ducks were swimming in the water. Some sort of a game was being played. The children seemed to be bouncing, as if they were balls, with each rebound higher than the one before. Some were doing flips and other acrobatic feats while in the air. The game appeared to be a follow-the-leader type of thing, and even the smaller ones were proficient in the gymnastics.

A little tug from Maggi reminded me that there was more here in the temple to investigate. Moving in toward the center, it was quieter, and the gentle power that I had felt earlier was stronger. Here were individuals, wise ones, it seems, stationed at intervals and waiting to assist those who chose to approach them.

I intuited that I should do so, and was strongly drawn to one on my right. Masculine in appearance with a flowing beard and very penetrating, knowing eyes, he was dressed in a robe of white. There was a band of gold encircling him—not in the form of what we might think of as an aura but more like a shiny ribbon of golden light. He gestured that I should sit before him, and I immediately heard his words in my mind. No verbalization was necessary.

"There is much you wish to know, and you shall. All information is available to you. We will assist and instruct, and then you may move to the center and receive it yourself. I already know your questions. Be assured that all will be answered. As you adjust and understand how to work with mind on this level, you will automatically know what is needed as the desire arises.

"You have wondered why you did not enter through the tunnel you have heard so much about. It is true that many experience their first awareness of this reality in that way, but when you separated from the body, you were immediately aware of the Light. You have been here before for brief periods and knew the way, so it was not necessary to travel through that corridor of mind known as the tunnel.

"The children you just saw are in your thoughts.

Surely you must have known that some would be here. They do not stay in that mode very long, for it is not the natural way of expression. When they come in, however, their mind-set is that they are a child of a certain age, and that is how they appear. We nurture and grow them gently into acceptance of adulthood. Then they are able to take full advantage of the wonderful opportunities for expansion on this level.

"Since your arrival here, you have been escorted through several different planes; there are many more, and nothing is restricted. Each person is free to experience fully, and the only governor is the state of the conscious mind. Deeply held beliefs are what come into visible expression here, just as they do on the dimension from which you have just come. Not everyone will have the same experience, for truly we create our own. However, subtle energies gently press on closed, restrictive minds, and like the rosebud's petals, they slowly open and expand and are soon willing to accept greater understanding. Then they are ready to move from their limited concept of life to the eternal adventure, for there is ever more to know, to do, to be.

"Know this: No one is lost or left behind. Each individual unit of consciousness is of equal importance and can never cease to exist. Whatever has been played out in the world of dense matter forms the initial mold for life here, but no one is locked into that mold, and each can progress to higher and higher levels of being.

"Be still and let me show you. There are cities out there as on the dense physical. Different levels of consciousness inhabit them. Observe. There are levels you would not feel comfortable on, but those who go there feel right at home."

Taking form before my eyes was the skyline of a great city. I could see three different dimensions of it simultaneously. The first had a dinginess pervading the atmosphere. There was a gloominess, and everything was gray, even the inhabitants, though I sensed that somewhere beneath the discoloration pulsed life and beauty. It brought to mind the lowest levels of existence in the world from which I'd come. Evil walked the squalid streets with malevolent bearing. No one here was up to, or expected, any good.

The second dimension was of the same panorama, but brighter and more colorful, and had a familiarity. Hope lived amid despair. There were neighborhoods with neat houses holding reasonably contented folk; shabby rows of dwellings housed those more discontented. Expansive lawns separated palatial homes from those of less grandeur. Within each sector was happiness and horror, love and hate, joy and sorrow—the dualities of life on a less than harmonious plane. It was a life accepted by many in the land I'd left behind as the only way life could be. Some knew better, more than just a few, and the hope that lived amid despair would at some time blossom into a better way of life.

Last in the trinity was a city of light, like unto John's holy city in the Book of Revelation. I saw the same skyline as before, but this time it was pure gold—with colors like precious gems, transparent glass, crystal clear. All who walked through the city brought glory and honor into it. Harmony and order prevailed, and the residents lived joyfully, creating that which brought forth beauty and fulfillment—a place of perfect peace, the peace that passeth understanding.

The slices of life I was seeing existed on both sides of the veil, I realized, and as I watched, the populations were shifting. A subtle but certain movement from the densest to the brightest was occurring. As misconceptions were altered on one level, a change took place on the next. Whether in physical form or on the other side of death, a change in perception benefited all. Truly our deeply held beliefs not only affect our own life experience but that of others. We are intricately connected to all that exists throughout eternity.

The Wise One continued speaking. "Throughout the vast unlimitedness of All That Is, the creative energy— that which is called the Spirit of God—is expressing itself as you, me, and everything else. Wherever we are, the God-source is, and we are always somewhere."

"Sometimes I am in places where God doesn't seem to be, as in the middle of a heart attack," I responded. "Surely God is not there."

"Yes. Wherever we are, the Source, God, is. A heart attack isn't bad. It is just an experience accepted on a certain level of being. We are so unlimited that we can limit, restrict, contract. Such power is awesome, for it is our very nature to create. We are constantly expressing in some way. Those who have chosen to move into the adventure of the dense matter we call physical must learn how fully to enjoy it. Physical is not lesser than other realms, just different. It is a special form of expression that has unique pleasures when we understand how to do it rightly. We should not be so eager to get out. Physical is not unspiritual. All is God. With understanding of omnipresence we will stop creating hurtful experiences, for fear will no longer exist. There is nothing wrong, nothing bad, there is just creation."

"Earlier I was shown how guilt eventually closed down my heart," I responded.

"Guilt is an offspring of fear and is most insidious. That tricky fellow works just below the surface of consciousness, feeding the fear that you have erred and usurping the power to express yourself freely lest you do something wrong and get into trouble. On the physical plane this is played out by the arteries becoming clogged; in your case a clot formed that closed off the flow of the lifeforce. On every level expression is restricted. See how it works. You are wondering what will happen when you go back in your body. The subconscious patterns were melted away by the Light, which will help in the healing of the physical. You can, in time, with right action, clear the pathways.

"Now go into the innermost part of the temple. You will find it easy there to open your mind and listen. Much knowledge will be received, but you will not be consciously aware of all of it at the moment. It will be assimilated and brought into remembrance bit by bit after you return to the body. More understanding is needed there, and you will have the opportunity to share. Beloved old friends will continue to work with you, as we have in the past."

I remembered the blessed time spent with teachers from another realm—Illuminati—during my meditations on the physical plane. I had somehow tapped into their energies, and their wise instruction helped me move to a higher level of awareness and understanding. They called themselves the "beloved old friends."

"Yes, I am one of them," he said. "This is why you were drawn to me. Remember what we have taught you and stay open to receive. Now go, for soon you must return. Our love is ever with you."

The sun is but a spark of fire,
a transient meteor in the sky; the soul immortal
as its sire, shall never die.
—*Robert Montgomery (1807–1855),*
English poet

6

In the Celestial Silence

I felt the warm radiance of that love as I stepped into the inner recesses of the temple—a beautiful arena of light. There was a soft glow of rosy gold, and it felt like a gentle massage, soothing and relaxing. Effortlessly, with no sense of hurry, I glided through varying shades of gold until the light was crystal-clear. Here, I was beyond thoughts; there was no analyzing—just an *experience* of being in the splendor.

I sat, quietly at ease, and had the sensation that tiny fingertips were caressing my crown. I felt my mind open like the petals of a flower. Then softly and tenderly came the knowingness, the connection with all that is. In moments of meditation I have touched this level before, but never with such completeness, clarity, intensity. Here, in this celestial silence, all was perfectly clear, understood. Here was fulfillment. All knowledge was mine, and I could draw it into conscious awareness as needed. On all levels we can tap into Universal

Mind, but it's easier here because of the more subtle energies.

A sweetness, an essence so pure, filled me, was me. This is what God is, all is, I am. With purity of heart I saw God and knew there is nothing else. I felt myself merging with, and ascending into, that crystalline brilliance. I touched true Joy, and I was lifted into the fullness of Being—the Essence of Life. In this glory I was free, and I beheld the Love that knows no conditions—the self-givingness of the Lifeforce we call God, ever nurturing and sustaining itself. All outlines disappeared, and there was no separation. Maintaining individual awareness, I was one with the Whole.

A remembrance comes—something I had written years ago about the experience of Oneness. Have I been here before? Of course! Otherwise how could I have described the unity of all that is in such detail? This is what I wrote five years before my heart attack:

In the center of the universe I stand encircled by Divine Being. In this I live and move and have my being. I am in this world, and of it. The world of natural order, ease, and joy. Eternal goodness flowing, doing, being all. There is only joy; waves of love support, sustain. I am in God, not outside.

I am in Love, consciously at peace with all there is. In God I love and move and have my being. In Love I live and move and have my being. In peace I live and move and have my being. There is nothing else. There is no outer. All is in the circle of God, Love, God Love. GOD LOVE.

The kingdom of God is within me. Yes. But more important, I am in the Kingdom of God. The Spirit of God is within me, but more important, I am in the Spirit of God. The Love of God is within me, but more important, I am in the Love of God. All there is is God. I can be nowhere else. I cannot be separate from God. There is nowhere else. There is no place else. There is no else. There only IS.

GODLOVE. It fills and sustains me. It is me. It is all, for it is all. I am that I am. No inner. No outer. Just IS. I am aware of all that is. I am all that is. In tune with the mighty flow of continuous expression, eternal being. Awake I am to the wonder of existence in this all-encompassing energy of ecstatic light, expansive love, eternal creation; ever-expanding, learning more of my omnipresent self.

I fly as the sparrow. I swim the clear waters encased in silvery fins. I am the mother and the newborn child, the father proud of his offspring. I experience the spectrum of love—loving, loved. I am filled with life, for I am that life. I run. I rest. I sleep and dream. I rise and see myself, the sun, rise also. The moonlight and the meadow, I am those; shining beams of moon lighting the night sky, gentle grasses moving in the breeze, the hoot of the owl in the tree nearby.

I am the cloud, the rock, the tree, the million grains of sand circling the deep blue sea. I express myself in many ways, as starry nights and sunny days. Through galaxies my spirit soars intent on being more and more.

There is no end to what I am. For I am God and God is me and there is nothing else to be.

I now understood more fully why we don't feel our Oneness with God moment to moment, constantly, while on the earth plane. We feel separated because of our physical bodies; we think we *are* the body and are therefore physical, yet we know that God is Spirit. Thus the sense of separation.

In both worlds there is nothing but energy, invisible and visible; we are spiritual beings wherever we may be. We are energy and God is energy, and energy cannot be broken up or separated. Born of God, we are spirit, and cannot be anything else. All is mind—one mind. We are that mind asleep—yet awakening, and God is that mind eternally aware.

Life beyond the veil is simply the continuity of life from one realm to another—death being only an entrance into fuller life, as a Wise One has said.

Now, before me, shimmering, iridescent light began to take a particular shape. A woman of breathtaking beauty appeared as I watched in awe, and even after the full materialization from pure light to visible, substantial form was complete, nothing was static. I continued to see a "quivering" of her structure, as though looking at a fluid, rippled reflection in a pond. Her movements were of pure grace as she positioned herself directly in front of me. Her hair was dark, her face pale, yet with color.

"Look into my eyes," she said with a gentle but commanding smile. As I did, I felt myself being absorbed. I was no longer just the entity I knew of as me, but more, so much more. The eyes I stared into were mine, the eyes of my soul.

In deep humility I accepted that which I was shown. "Oh my, I am all of that—so beautiful, glorious, wise, loving, kind, powerful. I didn't know. I had no idea."

As though looking into a kaleidoscope, I saw myriad lifetimes and experiences. Oh, the wonder of me. This powerful creative energy could take on any form it chose, and right now it was expressing as a woman called Jan, so of course I would perceive it as feminine.

Words from beyond my own thought processes began to pour into my mind. "You have been only casually thankful for your gift of life. Be thankful each day for this great gift. Most people go through life never really appreciating it. The purpose of life is joy, and with spiritual understanding the physical senses are enhanced. Savor fully the loveliness of each experience. Self-awareness is the prayer of the heart, and to pray without ceasing is to play. Play with the joyful abandon of the child, absorbed in the delight of each moment. Let go of obligation and duty, and live for the pure joy of being.

"Teach liberation. Fun and laughter are contagious, exposing all in their radius to the prosperous condition of happiness. Do what you really want to do. Follow the desires of your heart, and your blithe spirit will infect others. As you free yourself, your deeds and words will inspire others to break through the prison bars that have kept them from fulfillment. There is so much joy, so much good. Embrace it and express it, radiate and luxuriate in it.

"Take my hands," she said, and the sound of the voice was like music. As we made the connection, waves of ecstasy washed through me, and I took on the fullness of this magnificent being that I am an extension of. No longer was I observing this shimmering radiance. I was it. *The glory I had in the beginning,* I thought, *I have now and ever will have.* Complete in my individuality, I understood the old admonition "Know thyself."

A gentle pulling caught my attention, and I heard the melodic voice once more. *"Hold on to as much as you can as you make the descent back into the body and resume personality."*

I felt myself moving backward rapidly, feetfirst, as though I was being sucked into some vortex. Like a distant chime I heard the words, *"Remember, pray without ceasing. Play, love, laugh, live for the joy of it. Have fun. Happiness is holy."*

I had no power over the movement. I raced past groups of people dressed in white, and I recognized some of the faces. They waved and spoke to me, but I was moving so fast that I couldn't make out their words. I thought I saw my friend, Beth, and I wanted to stop and visit for a while, but I couldn't slow down. I was nearing the outer limits of that dimension, and my consciousness was beginning to register earth time. They continued to converse with me, but the picture was frozen, as though the pause button on the VCR had been pressed during a movie: They were inert, mouths open. I was out of sync with their "time."

As I approached the physical form, I passed five individuals who seemed to be assisting me. Maggi was still with me, and the last thing I remember seeing was her sweet face.

Back in the body, I was aware of sounds and John's face, but my mind was fuzzy. It was much clearer when I was out of the body.

Later, when I wrote my remembrance in my journal, I thought again of Dr. Stark's book, *A Doctor Goes to Heaven*. He wrote,

> Matter of earth was so gross by comparison to the substance of heaven, which was subtle and far more ethereal. There were similarities of structure, yet contrasts. . . . There were magnificent halls of records where one could discover when loved ones would be coming over. Other halls dealt with the unfolding of planetary history, so ancient that no work of earth dared to encompass such things. . . . In the center of the metropolis were buildings of indescribable beauty of structure . . . auditoriums for theater, sports and other activities. There were temples of such grandeur that it was breathtaking![1]

I also found it interesting that when I mentioned the Temple of Knowledge at a meeting of the International Association for Near-Death Studies, a woman excitedly raised her hand. I paused to let her speak, and she asked what it looked like.

"It's so clear in my mind that I could draw it," I said, and began to describe what I had seen. As I did, she nodded knowingly, and her eyes began to sparkle. "You went there too," I said.

"Yes," she replied.

I know what I experienced, but it is nice to hear from someone who has been to the same place. It's like telling a person that you stayed in a certain hotel in Paris, and they say, "I was there too—wasn't it wonderful?"

Then it becomes a shared experience, and very meaningful for both parties.

> Oh Lord, who lends me life,
> lend me a heart replete with thankfulness.
> —*William Shakespeare* (1564–1616),
> *English dramatist and poet*

7

Loving and Caring People

After my dramatic arrival at the hospital by helicopter and being met by the emergency-room welcoming committee, I should have realized that something really serious was going on—but in my semiconscious state, I was rather blasé.

As I mentioned earlier, when the doctor told me of the various procedures he felt were necessary, I thought, *I don't need to do that.* John remembers me shaking my head back and forth, as though I was saying no while he listened to Dr. Garza's menu. Apparently he paid no attention to me and gave him carte blanche—"Do whatever you have to, just fix her." And he did. Months later Dr. Garza laughingly told me that he'd never had anyone quite like me. "You were lying in a sea of hoses, smiling and saying, 'I'm just fine, I feel wonderful.'"

My hospital stay was quite pleasant. I was in intensive care for several days, and the care *was* intensive. Sweet, loving nurses were attentive to my every need.

Cookie was there the first night settling me in. Then dear Fran was with me most of the rest of the time. There were others, as well as the various technicians who stopped by from time to time. All were kind and caring.

The attention didn't stop when I was moved to a regular room. Having spent little time in hospitals, I was surprised at the high degree of skill and compassion of the people I encountered. Even the food was good, except for the funny eggs. I told John that it was almost like being at a spa. Note that I said "almost."

This adventure began on a Thursday, and after the death scene at our house I was pretty much in and out of consciousness the rest of the day. Early Friday morning I noticed a clock on the wall I was facing; it was ten minutes to six. I remembered that it was December 31st, and all over the world people were gathering for the annual World Healing Day—a global mind-link that takes place at noon Greenwich time. That's six A.M. in Texas.

I tuned in and let words from the beautiful meditation my husband wrote for this event come to mind, and with a grateful heart sent forth my prayer for the healing and harmonizing of this planet and all forms of life hereon: "Let peace come forth in every mind. . . . Let love flow forth from every heart. . . . Let forgiveness reign in every soul. . . . Let understanding be the common bond."

A group of people were meeting in our office for the

mind-link, with breakfast following. I knew Jack and Laura, my office cohorts, would take care of it. They did—and that wasn't all. For weeks to come they took over the activities that were usually mine to do. Everything worked so smoothly that I've never fully resumed my previous role. I didn't want to, for I knew my life must be different now.

John and Susan arrived and we had some time together before I was taken back to "cold storage"—that ice-cold operating room. The doctors did another heart cath to see how things were progressing, and then removed the tube. From what I heard later, my heart was operating at 90 percent, compared to 10 percent the night before. The doctor was very pleased with my return to near normalcy so quickly. It was probably due to all those prayers, as well as the fact that I'd hardly ever experienced any kind of illness before.

The rest of the day is kind of blurry, probably because of the drugs they fed me to keep me from feeling the goings-on in the cold-storage department. Little blips of remembrance did occur from time to time, such as the out-of-body experience above the stretcher. John and I talked about it. He told me what he had observed while the EMS team was working on me, and things got clearer.

Saturday was New Year's Day, and I was still in intensive care. Somehow John managed to sneak in four of our close friends, then pulled the curtain around us to hide everyone. Our daughter Susie was there too. We laughed and talked for almost an hour until the nurse said they had to go (though I think the nurses knew all along and decided to let us have a little fun). During the "party" one of our friends said, "I've never known anyone who died and came back. What was it like over there?" The color blue and the golden light flooded my mind, and I remembered feeling that I was in a holding pattern. Then flashes of recollections, but so brief I couldn't discuss them. The experience was sacred to me, and I didn't feel comfortable talking about it until the events were completely clear in my mind. Later, as the flashes connected and the scenes became vivid, I felt that I could share my observations with others.

One thing everyone wanted to know was what I had looked like. To be honest, I don't know. I never thought about it, but I did have a body—arms, legs, head, and so forth. My body had seemed lighter. I think I must have looked much as I do now. The people I saw looked much like those from the physical world, though there was a glow about them. It's not that you get an-other body; it's more like you shed the one you've been wearing and another one you already have is revealed— like changing clothes.

That Saturday night, January 1st, my darling husband came back to the hospital alone. He said, "I can't stand it any longer. I have to hold you and feel you close to me." He climbed into the bed and we managed to hold each other without dislodging any of my connections. Tears flowed as he let out his fears and feelings, and we clung to each other in gratitude that we could.

Looking back, John recalled the sequence of events:

"*It's interesting how our emotions work. On the day of the heart attack, when we were discussing how she felt, I was concerned about her, but not overly so. But while we were waiting for EMS, I became very impatient, antsy, wanting her to be taken care of without further delay. The tension was mounting right up to the point when I saw her die on the stretcher and heard the words 'We've lost her.' Maybe it was the shock, but suddenly nothing seemed to intrude upon my conscious awareness or feeling nature. My mind registered no response—no horror, fear, grief—nothing. I had shifted into another state of consciousness best described as totally detached and completely impersonal. In fact I remember 'seeing' her in my mind as whole, complete, radiantly healthy—with absolutely nothing wrong with her body—as the words* Life! Life! Life! *were silently spoken, but without any sense of urgency.*

"*The detachment remained as I helped carry the EKG machine to the ambulance, came back into the house to find Jan's purse, and drove to the high school where the helicopter would land. Then on the way into town, the emotional roller coaster began, slowly at first, then picked up steam through the day, the night, and the following morning—until I knew for sure that she was going to be all right.*

"*All that I wanted to do then was cry. I hadn't done that yet. And by Saturday afternoon I felt that I would explode and fall apart unless I held her close to me and*

released—through flowing tears—all the feelings that
had been suppressed. I needed a healing, and she
helped me do that. And when I drove home that night,
I knew that both of us were beginning a new life together.
The anger, the second part of the grief process, would
come later."

Susie had come in on Friday, so she had seen me and talked to me, and knew that I was okay. But Leslie was so far away, and we knew she wasn't sure that all was well. After Leslie had called several times, the nurse in intensive care brought the phone to me so that I could talk to her. I think that was the first time she really believed I was all right.

My daughters are very precious to me, and we are blessed with a close relationship. Only a few months before this event we'd gone to France to play with Leslie and see her new environs. We had such fun, and I could hardly wait to go back. (Dr. Garza said I'd have to wait until I could say *heart attack* in French, and be sure that I was understood.)

Interestingly everyone else was more concerned about me than I was. I knew that I was just fine, and felt a complete sense of ease and contentment. It was easy to let go and allow others to take care of everything. I had no worries or concerns.

Flowers began to arrive—each day more and more. There were so many that when it was time to go home, I asked if some could be shared with others who might need some cheer. Then when I got home, I found more.

Two special friends brought a beautiful little angel to watch over me, and cards and letters poured in from all over the world. How did they know? Through the prayer network that Laura at our office had contacted, and the word quickly spread.

Home from the hospital, it was easy to let John do things for me that I would have felt guilty about before. He did the shopping, cooked the meals, and pampered me in every way imaginable. I felt a complacence, a placidity, so I was very content to be at ease and do little. I followed the instructions of the doctor and Methodist Hospital's wonderful cardiac rehabilitation program, doing mild exercises and beginning a walking program that would build weekly.

A week after I left the hospital, John was scheduled to give a talk in San Antonio on the theme of positive living. I went with him and sat in the front row. He was doing just fine, but right in the middle of his speech he looked down and saw me. He forgot everything he was going to say and immediately began telling the crowd about my experience—going into great dramatic detail. He got a standing ovation. Later he said the applause was for me, not him. Maybe it was for both of us, because we had gone through everything together, and in some ways the experience was tougher on him.

How do I feel since the experience? In the beginning, actually for the first few months, I felt insulated— almost as though I were in a protective cocoon, untouched by outer circumstances—in the world but not of it, completely enfolded in love. I was not my usual loquacious self. "In quietness and confidence shall be your strength" is a true statement, for I found an inner strength, an assurance, greater than I'd known before: content with myself, who I am, how I am . . . glad to be me, here, now. Feeling complete, I had no need to speak a lot. It was good to be still, and know.

That doesn't mean that I just sat around and led a sedentary life. John and I joined a health club, walking miles on the treadmill every day and lifting weights. And I resumed my normal activities—but with a difference. I did things for the joy of it, and I played more, with a different view of life and living.

I think death is most interesting because it makes you think a lot about life. If you die and come back, at first you think about what it was like "over there." Then you think about how great it is here. Then you wonder if you'll be able to stay as long as you might like. You remember how easy it was to get out, and you seemed to have no control over the transition—it just happened.

When I was out, I didn't care. Now that I'm back in, I don't want to get out again for a while. I don't want to waste my time here. I want to go places and do things. I want to live life fully, and I don't know how long I've got. No one gave me a schedule or timetable.

I know John wants to make every moment count. He's rarely planned anything special for his birthday, but that particular February celebration, six weeks after my hospital stay, was quite different. He arranged for a suite at a fine hotel in San Antonio—one offering "luxury and intimacy"—made reservations at a continental restaurant, and called two other couples—close friends—to join us for dinner. Later that night, on *his* birthday, he gave me a gift—a beautiful red silk robe and nightgown. And as he wrote about it later,

"We let the air be charged with the lovely fragrance of delightful romance. The next day we saw San Antonio in a completely different way. It was no longer an old, crowded city—it was a jewel, a gem of beauty and charm, filled with wonderful, happy people expressing life and love. We shopped as tourists, laughed with the vendors, skipped along the River Walk waving at the smiling faces in the boats, smelled the gorgeous flowers, listened to the music, ate like starving kids, and had a magnificent time."

We were learning to play.

Later that month, I gave a workshop called "Freedom Flight." It had been planned six months before, but considering my recent experience, I thought the title was very appropriate. Afterward John and I flew to Puerto Vallarta, that fabulous gem on the Pacific coast of Mexico. We stayed in a condo right on the beach, which had been recommended by a friend. In fact, he came over to our home one evening before our departure to bring us a map of the town and a list of the best gourmet restaurants. We hit them all—great French cuisine.

During the day, we dozed on the sand in the sun,

dipped in the salty waves, walked a four-mile stretch, and became terribly spoiled by our white-shirted waiter from the nearby restaurant, who constantly provided snacks and drinks.

John recalled the trip:

"*Do dreams come true? They sure do. Before we left, I had been thinking about dancing until the wee hours of the morning with this love of mine. Well, we went to one place near the beach for a late-evening dinner— not knowing we could dance there—and suddenly the music was playing. We danced hard and soft rock and everything in between, and then they played a love song. If there was anyone else on the dance floor, we didn't see them.*"

This is what I wrote later about that magic moment: "Warm tears sliding down my cheeks as we danced. No sadness, just deep feeling for the experience of the moment . . . together, touching, expressing our love for each other with the rhythmic movement of our bodies. I lift my head and look into his eyes, and I see my love for him echoed back to me. Tears of joy we shed together as we dance. Joyful gratitude for this opportunity to be in physical form together at this time. To touch, and feel, and love—to savor our livingness, to express our thankfulness by living life to the fullest . . . forever, forever, forever."

I think "Forever" was the name of the song they were playing.

8

A Look at Death

How do I feel about death? It is usually described as a cessation of life. But that can't be true, because you cannot destroy life—it's eternal. A pause between parentheses? No, not even a pause. "The spirit of God has made me, and the breath of the Almighty gives me life" (Job 33:40), and nothing can cut the breath of God short. We are eternal beings because God is.

As John wrote in *The Angels Within Us*, "In truth that which we call death is but an entrance into a more glorious life of joy, fulfillment, peace, and freedom, whether the experience is physical or mystical. In each case it is an unceasing flow of sentient life, but with a difference. Except for the immediate uplift of consciousness derived from the experience of being freed from the corporeal body, physical death is nothing more than a change in form. We maintain the awareness, understanding, and knowledge gained during our visit on earth and carry our tendencies and interests with us as we move from one plane to another."[1]

I don't think either one of us has ever believed in death as an end to life. We were created to live for the joy of it on every plane of existence, and the only death is when the light of joy is extinguished. Maybe that's where the word *zombie* came from—people in "a state of trancelike animation"—the sorrowful walking-dead of this world.

In *A Course in Miracles* we read, "Death is the symbol of the fear of God. His Love is blotted out in the idea, which holds it from awareness like a shield held up to obscure the sun. The grimness of the symbol is enough to show it cannot coexist with God. . . . If death is real for anything, there is no life. Death denies life. But if there is reality in life, death is denied. No compromise in this is possible. There is either a god of fear or One of Love. . . . He did not make death because He did not make fear. Both are equally meaningless to Him."[2]

To me this says once again that God did not author death. We did. It was our idea, which means it carries little weight in the cosmic scheme of things. "For I have no pleasure in the death of him that dieth, saith the Lord God: wherefore turn yourselves, and live ye" (Ezekiel 18:32). The Almighty gave us Life everlasting, which is the opposite of death, and we were created out of Love— the opposite of fear. The fact is God doesn't deal in opposites. That's why death and fear are not part of the Creator's vocabulary. They shouldn't be in ours either.

Even in the title of the great religious book of ancient Egypt, *The Book of the Dead*, the word that translates as *dead* actually means "the day of making manifest one's godhood."[3] And to the ancient Greek philosophers, the departure from the physical plane was actually a *birth*: "The only true birth was that of the spiritual soul of man rising out of the womb of his own fleshly nature."[4]

Maybe we can't escape the use of the word *death* in everyday language, but hopefully we can at least understand that it means something else besides "the end of us."

In a newspaper column the Reverend Billy Graham wrote, "He [God] has told us that this life is not all there is and that death is not the end of us. Instead, death is only a transition, and after death every person will enter eternity, either in heaven with God or in hell separated from God."[5] Yet since God is omnipresent, we know that truly we can never be separated from God. However, if that is not our awareness, understanding, and knowledge, we may certainly seem to experience a sense of separation. In time that, too, will pass.

In the book *Esoteric Healing* by Alice Bailey we find the following: "The fear and horror of death is founded upon the love of form—our own form, the forms of those we love and the form of our familiar surroundings and environment. . . . The hope of the future, and the hope of our release from this ill-founded fear, lie in the shifting of our emphasis to the fact of the eternal soul and to the necessity for that soul to live spiritually, constructively and divinely within the material vehicles."[6]

We're not talking about a person's loss of life when we refer to death; rather we're referring to a physical body that stops functioning. But we are not physical bodies. We are endless, immortal consciousness. We *have* a body to animate and communicate with and be recognized by, but we aren't it. In another book Bailey goes on to say, "Just as long as our consciousness is identified with the [body], death will hold for us its ancient terror. Just as soon as we know ourselves to be souls, and find that we are capable of focusing our consciousness or sense of awareness in any form or any plane at will, or in any direction within the form of God, we shall no longer know death."[7]

Our body vehicle is filled with potent energy that gives it life. When the lifeforce is withdrawn and the body is an empty shell, we call that death. Much grief and emotion are a part of this physical experience, for there is fear that this is all. The empty body shell reminds us of the personality that once inhabited it, and we focus on the emptiness and feel loss. If we directed our attention to the lifeforce that inhabited the body, we would realize that life still is. Life Is. It's as simple as that. Life cannot be death. As Bailey says, "We are conscious one moment on the physical plane, and a moment later we have withdrawn onto another plane and are actively conscious there."[8]

The mighty energy that fills us at birth is still existing through another birth we call death—a new experience in a different form. There is a cycle of continuance, a coming in and a going out of the physical plane. But this plane is only one of many. We were not meant to stay here forever. We just forgot how to go out without leaving our physical body behind. Then when we saw all those bodies lying around, we conceived the idea of death; no life was in them, so they were empty—dead.

It's my feeling that instead of dropping the body, we're supposed to alter its molecular structure and take its energy with us when we leave. But with the feelings of separation we forgot how, and this would explain why there is so much sadness surrounding what we call death. Someday we'll remember how to change the energy vibration.

We know, somewhere down deep, that the body is a *part* of all of us, the physical manifestation of the Spirit of God. Charles Fillmore, cofounder of Unity, wrote that "the body is the outer form of the thoughts, and it therefore could not die or disintegrate unless a similar process had first taken place on the mental plane."[9] So in our mind we are denying the reality of our spiritual selfhood. We are forgetting that Spirit lowers its vibration to the dense physical level of form, but that it is still Spirit.

The Bible said Jesus died, simply meaning that he left that fleshly body. Then, because he knew how, he changed the pattern of movement of the electrons and altered the atomic structure of matter that was his physical body so that it was no longer visible. "That which I can do you can do also." And we will.

In *The Mystery of Death and Dying,* Earlyne Chaney writes about this altering of the body:

> Such a form would need to be consistently pure, the atoms vibrating at an accelerated voltage of electromagnetic power. . . . The soul would be in total command of the sympathetic nervous system, controlling automatic functions and manipulating the form to suit the soul's mission on Earth.
>
> Jesus possessed such a form. More than once he caused it to disappear when he was surrounded by his enemies.
>
> At any rate, this seems to be one status of future immortality—so that certain light bringers, having perfected a physical form, could at will transmute it into the substances of *all* the planes and dwell on any vibratory level requiring their presence, from the physical to the celestial.[10]

Till then we'll leave the vacated body here to disintegrate slowly, but even that substance will return to the unformed to manifest as something new. No one stays confined in matter forever. Why would we want to?

The sides of death are not that separate; life resides in both places. In 1990 a dear friend was hospitalized with what we call a terminal illness. I saw her lying in a hospital bed. "She is dying," the doctors said. Over, in, and through that body I saw a lighter, finer body sitting up, laughing, singing, vibrant. My friend was not dying. She is living and always will live. She may get out of the physical vehicle and walk away, but she will continue to live.

Paul wrote in 1 Corinthians: "There is a natural body, and there is a spiritual body." Then, "Death is swallowed up in victory. O death, where is thy sting? O grave, where is thy victory?"

And Ernest Holmes, founder of the Religious Science movement, wrote, "Death has nothing to do with life everlasting, and is but an impatient gesture of the soul, wishing to rid itself of a body no longer useful."[11]

As we can see, there is no such thing as death, the end of life, or the "final curtain." Death is nothing more than a transition, which means passage, transformation. As the esteemed American philosopher Manly P. Hall states it, "Death seems a dismal and ultimate expression, when it actually signifies simply transition and is in no way concerned with a belief in a beginning or a fear of end."[12] Hall also writes that "death is regarded as a change of condition, when, in reality, it is only a change of place."[13] I know this is true, and that's why we grieve. The person has gone to another place. But where?

Where is this other place? George Meek, researcher of the paranormal and author of *After We Die, What Then?* described six of the infinite number of planes on the other side, then asked, "Where are these planes, levels or 'mansions' actually located? Are they in some far-off part of the universe or cosmos?

"Strange and unbelievable as it may seem, the Nazarene was telling the literal truth when He said, 'The

Kingdom of Heaven is *within* you!' He was not speaking in parables."[14] Meek goes on to say that heaven and the many mansions are indeed within each one of us as interpenetrating levels of life and consciousness.

Joseph Campbell says basically the same thing: "We know that Jesus could not have ascended to heaven because there is no physical heaven anywhere in the universe. Even ascending at the speed of light, Jesus would still be in the galaxy. Astronomy and physics have simply eliminated that as a literal, physical possibility. But if you read 'Jesus ascended to heaven' in terms of its metaphoric connotation, you see that he has gone inward—not into outer space but into inward space, to the place from which all being comes, into the consciousness that is the source of all things, the kingdom of heaven within."[15]

The Great Beyond is not out or up, but *in*—in you and me and everyone else—right where we are at this moment. In our three-dimensional way of thinking this may be difficult to grasp, but the other side of death is simply another dimension, and the door to that dimension is within our individual energy fields. It is a "secret place"—a cosmic longitude and latitude in deep inner consciousness—an energy vortex through which we pass to the world of heaven, a world closer than breathing. Now we can understand why those who have passed over can still seem to be so close to us. They are.

On the death of his son a friend asked Socrates, "Why do you weep? It will not bring him back."

"That is why I weep," replied Socrates.

This attitude toward death will change in time. As the wisdom teachings tell us, "An entirely new concept of death, with the emphasis upon conscious withdrawal, will be taught, and funeral services, or rather the crematory services, will be joyous events because their emphasis will be upon release and return."[16] In the meantime we must learn how to handle grief in a more constructive way.

In her wonderful book *Seven Choices* Elizabeth Harper Neeld, Ph.D., gives us a map of the complete grieving process. She writes, "Having experienced a series of losses . . . I have reflected much on the mourning process. I've had much opportunity to halt and to bungle my own progress, because for so long I didn't understand how to grieve. I've had much opportunity to learn, often by trial and error, what works to bring mourning to a constructive conclusion."[17]

Dr. Neeld tells us that we must move from the initial impact of loss, where we express grief fully, to what she calls "the second crisis," where "we let ourselves be exposed to the truth about what we have lost." From there her map takes us to where we can look honestly at the situation, make a turn, and choose to take action to work through the conflict, continuing to make choices until we achieve freedom from "the domination of grief."

This freedom involves moving past both fear and anger. Not a simple task, because even with an understanding of the continuance of life, dealing with our emotions can be hard. And it is doubly difficult to bring comfort to another who is going through the experience, especially if he or she has not considered the idea that life exists on many planes.

John agrees.

"*I* do know that life continues," he says, "but the internal shock of seeing Jan die, followed by the emotional roller coaster on that day and night, left a powerful residue that would erupt later. About a month after she came home from the hospital, we were asleep in bed and I woke up, thinking that I'd heard her make a sound. 'Are you all right?' I asked. When she didn't answer, I shook her firmly and repeated the question.

"She turned over and said, 'Of course I'm all right. Why did you wake me up to ask that question?'

"Suddenly the volcano erupted. I felt a rage that I'd never experienced before. I leaped out of bed, walked out of the bedroom and down the hall like a soldier hell-bent for war, and proceeded to destroy, with fists and feet, the door leading to another room. For several minutes I let out every pent-up emotion—all the grief, fear, and anger (how could she dare leave me?) that had been suppressed. Then I went downstairs to my study and cried.

"Half an hour later I felt her presence and looked up to see her peeking around the door. 'Now it's my turn to ask the question,' she said. 'Are you all right?' I held out my arms and she came to me and we cried together.

"We never know what grief has hidden down there

*in the subterranean chambers of mind. Fortunately I
was able to release the steam in the boiler through a physical
encounter with a door, and bring about the needed closure."*

Several years ago I wrote in my journal after a conversation with my daughter, who was dealing with the
loss of a close friend: We are mourning the loss of ourselves. As one leaves [dies], we no longer feel complete,
and all our unhappiness becomes centered in the loss of
this one who is no longer with us. A part of us seemingly no longer exists. If part of me goes so easily,
maybe all of me can. I feel the hurt of others and cannot reach them—the hurt separates and I am angry at
the power that lets this be. Why must we hurt? If there
is no death, we should know and not feel loss or hurt or
fear or separation. I must not die within because I do
not understand why someone else has gone. I still have
this life to live, and through living may come to better
understand the unanswered WHY?

The great philosophers of the past wrote much about
life being a readying for death—that we should always
be prepared to die. But how many of us are? A few years
ago I decided to fly to visit my mother and had an experience that brought this question to mind, along with
many realizations.

The night before I was to leave, I began to feel uneasy about the trip. I felt as though something was out
of order and that for some reason I wasn't coming back.
My mind dismissed this as my not wanting to go, for
there were many other things I wanted to do back at

home. The next morning the feeling was very strong, and I took it into my meditation to release it, but I still felt a disturbance. My intuition did not say "don't go," but there was an awareness of disharmony. The feeling lifted on the way to the airport, and I boarded the plane with no qualms whatsoever.

The first leg of the trip was uneventful, and I changed planes in Dallas. There was to be one stop between Dallas and my destination, and the plane took off without delay. As we approached the interim stop and prepared for landing, the plane circled the airport many times. Before long the pilot announced that we were going back to Dallas. He said that the instruments did not indicate that the landing gear was locked, and the small airport was not equipped for an emergency landing.

Emergency procedures began: Get acquainted with the person next to you and be sure he gets off the plane. Locate the nearest exit on each side of the plane. Practice the position to be assumed at landing—your head on your knees and your arms under the knees grasping the elbows.

As we got closer to Dallas, the flight attendants suggested that we remove all jewelry and shoes with heavy heels. This was beginning to feel real—we were definitely going to have an emergency landing. I spoke silently to God: *I really don't feel ready to go; it seems there is so much more for me to do here. But if my mission is complete, it's okay. If not, Guardian Angels, surround this plane!*

Then came the announcement from the cockpit to assume the crash position. As the plane began to descend, I simply said, *God, this is in your hands*. Over and over in my mind as the plane approached the runway, I thought . . . *God, God, God*. Oddly I felt that whatever was going to happen was all right.

Suddenly we were on the ground and the pilot announced that everything was fine. As I sat up and looked out the window, I could see fire trucks and all kinds of emergency equipment. I felt a great sense of relief, and I noticed that the top of my head and face were soaking wet but the rest of my body was perfectly dry. Then I realized that the spiritual energy I was invoking with my silent words had been pouring into the energy center of the crown, generating intense heat.

Why was I on the plane? Why did I have the premonition? Whatever the reasons, I was supposed to be there. I know that. I learned many things from this experience, one of which was that I wasn't afraid of leaving my body, of what we call death. I experienced faint feelings of regret, of not having finished all I wanted to do, but no fear. "Lo, though I walk through the valley of the shadow of death, thou art with me." It is true. The Presence of God is everpresent, before and after birth, on each side of the physical spectrum.

Rodney Collin, who has thoroughly researched the cosmic mysteries, highlights an interesting facet of the death process in terms of its relationship to the sex act. He says,

Many analogies—both physical and psychological—suggest that sexual ecstasy, in which opposites are reconciled, in which the sense of union is in proportion to the sense of annihilation, and in which one seems both to lose oneself and find oneself at once, may be a true foretaste of what may be expected in death.

At the same time, in sexual union man and woman themselves unknowingly create a cosmic image of the whole. The separate halves, divorced since the dawn of life, become for a moment one perfect creature, its eyes looking to earth and sky at once, the rhythm of its two hearts united, breathing its own breath, fulfilling its own yearnings, and completing its own incompleteness—a new creature purged of evil and of self, and filled with a single ecstasy, the image of a cosmos in its perfection.[18]

I've given some thought to what Collin wrote, and I believe that his parable on the relationship of death and sex is meaningful, particularly when you consider that both truly represent a union of completeness. I know that in dying I experienced the ecstasy, the surrender and discovery of my perfect self, and the conscious reuniting with my soul. And equating our passing with the climax of sexual excitement certainly does remove the fear of death.

There is no death! What seems so is transition;
this life of mortal breath is but a suburb of the life elysian,
whose portal we call death.
—*Henry Wadsworth Longfellow (1807–1882),*
American poet

9
Life Continues

T he old hymns sung by the voices from the church of my childhood frequently come to mind. They tell about the beautiful dwelling place prepared for us on the other side, with fresh young trees and flowers that never fade, where life continues eternally. Long before the term "near-death experience" was coined, people knew there was something beyond this physical life. They were right.

Marcus Caldwell told his gifted wife, writer Taylor Caldwell, as he lay dying that if there was an afterlife, he would come back and give her a sign. He made his transition, and three days later Taylor's housekeeper summoned her out to the backyard. Still numb with grief, she looked with amazement. Blooming for the first time in twenty-one years was a shrub of resurrection lilies. Marcus had said many times that proof of the Resurrection certainly wasn't in those lilies. But, bare the day before, the plant had burst into a blaze of glorious white blooms.

The financial officer of a large automobile dealership heard of my quick trip to paradise and said to me, "It's there, isn't it, Jan?" He had been there, too, and once you have, you don't forget it. The memory he retained was of all that love and of being surrounded by a group of people who came to meet him.

With tears streaming down her face, a woman told of leaving her body when her heart stopped and seeing her father who spoke to her. He had been ill many years prior to his death, but was now standing young and well before her. Deeply touched by her experience, she wanted to tell others, but found that not everyone was receptive.

My friend Jean tells of her near-death experience in 1981: "I first went to a light spot and the ground area was fluffy white clouds and everything was white. I was alone and knew it was a place to come into alignment. It was a very comfortable place, and from there I just slipped through the cloud floor to an area where I saw my father. And then I returned."

Yes, "it's there"—and more and more of us are returning from brief visits to tell about it, so many that an organization has been formed called the International Association for Near-Death Studies.

That we returned from the dead seems to bother some people. The director of a religious organization in Houston was quoted as saying, "Traditional Christianity is hesitant to get embraced by that light. There is dislike, too, in Judaism and in Christianity about contact with the dead. They just don't get involved with the dead. Leave that to God." But that's not what I heard in that little Baptist church in the small town where I grew up, where beautiful souls sang about life beyond the veil.

And Christians not getting involved with the dead? That's not what the Bible teaches. We all know the Lazarus story, and also the account in three of the books of the New Testament in which Jesus met with Moses and Elias on Mount Herman. They were observed by Peter, James, and John, who had gone there with him to pray.

Matthew 17:2–3 says, "And [Jesus] was transfigured before them and his face did shine as the sun, and his raiment was white as the light. And, behold, there appeared unto them Moses and Elias talking with him." A similar description in Mark 9:3–4: "And his raiment became shining, exceeding white as snow: so as no fuller on earth can white them. And there appeared unto them Elias with Moses: and they were talking with Jesus." Luke 9:29–30 tells it this way: "And as he prayed, the fashion of his countenance was altered, and his raiment was white and glistening. And, behold, there talked with him two men, which were Moses and Elias."

It amazes me that people object to the deeply meaningful experiences so many have had, whether called near-death, out-of-body, visionary, or something else. We report a beautiful, loving continuation of life, yet there are those who feel they must prove our experiences false. I would think folks would be glad to hear the joyful news, the good news, that life continues, all is "forgiven," there is more and more to experience, that that which we call God is benevolent, that the creative force of the universe does not work against itself.

A Gallup poll in 1982 found that about eight million American adults claimed having near-death experiences. That was over a decade ago and didn't include children. Our numbers are increasing, and the message we return with is God is Good! How wonderful that there is no condemning, judgmental, hateful deity who sometimes punishes, sometimes rewards, and whom we must live in constant fear of displeasing. The Great IS loves me as It loves Itself, for I am included in that vastness, that immenseness, that indivisible Being. No one can take away what I now know, and I *do* know. And so does Edward, whom I met at a meeting of the International Association for Near-Death Studies. Here's his story:

Driving home on December 30, 1969, in Atlanta, Georgia, my car crashed into a large oak tree. I felt myself propelled into the "veins" of the tree and popped out of the top, as a bubble would rise to the surface of water.

Looking down at the scene below me, as if I were on a second-story balcony, I saw a car smashed against the tree, smoke and steam coming out from under the hood, and people running out the door of a nearby house. As I looked closer at the images below me, I saw a body slumped over the steering wheel, blood pouring out of its head.

That's my car, I thought. Then I realized, *That's my body!* As I formed the question *If that's my body . . . then who/what am I?* I was instantly removed from that whole scene as if by a vacuum. I found myself cascading down a long, dark, twisting tunnel. A tiny light, like a star in the sky, appeared in the distance.

Quickly I found myself surrounded by the most intense and wonderful light. It was so soothing, elevating, enlightening, and relieving. I am frustrated by the limits of language to convey this experience. It was, and is, the most euphoric ecstasy of body, mind, and spirit that anyone can ever know.

In the next scene (time became irrelevant) a figure came forward from the surrounding light. It appeared to be the image of Jesus as I had visualized him when I was growing up as an altar boy in the Episcopal church. His presence radiated a peace and love beyond description. I was in rapture.

He reached toward me with his right hand as I heard (in my head and mind—not my ears), "Welcome, we've been waiting for you." With his left hand he pointed back to a figure seated a short distance away. Reluctantly I pulled my concentration away from his beaming smile and looked where he was pointing. There, sitting on a throne, was this gentle, beautiful, glorious being. He looked like Santa, or a grandfather—a God Father—FATHER GOD. I felt awed by his grace, peace, and radiating joy. He waved to me, beckoning me to come with his right hand, patting his knee with his left hand.

For the first time I became SELF conscious. Like a child, I retreated with, "Who, me?" In the next instant I found myself in God's lap with his arm supporting me as I gazed into his eyes in even more ecstasy. Pointing toward something at his feet with his right hand, he conveyed the question "Are you through?"

Reluctantly following his implied command, I turned from drinking in the love of his smile to examine the images that lay at his feet. Like so many small TV screens lined up in a semicircle below me were scenes from my life. As I focused on each one, I instantly relived it.

There I was, four or five years old, stealing Coke bottles from a neighbor's garage. I reexperienced the musty smell. I felt the excited, anxious pounding of my heart. I heard the clinking of the bottles. I recalled the smug satisfaction of thinking, *Aha, I got away with it.* As the episode faded, I realized I was still in God's lap. I said, "Oh, oh, that's bad. I'm sorry." Shame and embarrassment filled me. God's response stunned me to my core. He said, "That's neither good nor bad. Are you through?"

Commanded by his grace, I continued to review the scenes of my life. In every case, whether I was proud of some "good" or ashamed of some "bad," the response was the continual outpouring of unconditional love. God conveyed, "It's neither good, nor bad. It is a lesson. Are you through?" (Another scene) "That's neither good nor bad. Are you through?"

I got to see that there are no secrets when we die.

Also, the only judgment is that which we have within ourselves.

"Am I through?" I thought. There is no way I wanted to go back into the life of doubt, fear, shame, and attachments. Looking down at my life from God's lap, I had the thought *I'll be complete once I let my mom know I'm okay.* I came to in a hospital bed, dazed, aching all over, and transformed for life. Two weeks had passed, and Mom was there at the foot of the bed waiting for me and welcoming me back.

According to the January–February 1995 issue of *The Woodrew Update*,

> *The European* of London reported that Drs. van Lommel and van Wees recently concluded a four-year study of cardiac patients at 10 Dutch hospitals that they are calling "the first genuinely scientific study of near-death experiences." One in five of the 345 patients interviewed gave graphic accounts of events that occurred while they were observed clinically dead. The study has attracted a great deal of interest worldwide because of its "advanced methodology and rigorously scientific approach." They are saying that "for the first time in NDE research, clinical death was clearly defined and accurately timed." Those patients who were then resuscitated were interviewed as soon as possible. The team followed up with in-depth interviews a year later to determine whether the experience had affected their lives. . . . The 49 men and 13 women reported the *same* classic experiences that Kenneth Ring and Up-

dater author P.M.H. Atwater have been reporting for years.

The number of excellent books written about NDEs should have been sufficient to convince any open-minded reader of their validity. It is therefore very nice to involve the minds of the many who will *only* believe in NDEs through the rigorous scientific approach of the Dutch studies.[1]

Let's look now at the case of P. in California, who died but couldn't get past the door at the end of the tunnel. Here's her report:

I had left my body several times as a child. I would get very ill with very high temperature. When I couldn't stand any more pain, I would go up in the corner and watch my body on the bed, then I would go back in and repeat the process whenever necessary.

When I was thirty years old, my heart stopped and I was technically dead. I was in the hospital and I left my body and watched all the action from up in the corner of the room. I could see everyone working frantically on my body. Then I was suddenly in a tunnel of very intense bright light, very warm, totally penetrating. There was a high-pitched sound, also a hum. I was in the shape of my body but transparent. It was the most wonderful feeling I've ever had. I *knew* that I was loved, that I was free, that I was going home. *I was happy!*

I was traveling at what seemed a great speed, and I knew that I was going to go out of this tunnel to something bigger. But just at the end of the tunnel my three small children were standing there looking very sad, and I knew that I couldn't continue my trip at that time. When that thought went through my mind, the doors at the end of the tunnel closed with a great noise—but the doors were not long vertical ones like house doors, they were horizontal. For some reason that has always been very vivid in my memory.

I was suddenly back in the emergency room at the hospital looking at my body and knowing what I had to do—and I did it. It didn't fit very well, but I adjusted. I'm still in it and I'm fifty-three years old now. I don't fear death as a result of this trip. I think it was a special gift to show me, and I do wish that everyone could know that there really is nothing to be afraid of. It is total love and freedom—it was wonderful. I've had experiences when I was a child, so I always knew that there are a lot more things around than what we saw as humans.[2]

I've been asked questions such as "Why did you have this experience? Were you chosen for some special reason?" The only thing special is that I remembered it. Everyone who dies must experience *something*, though for some reason the memory may not be retained. Perhaps their belief system blocks it out because it is unacceptable to their way of thinking. Or maybe they're so frightened by leaving their bodies that they don't want to remember. For whatever reason, we don't always recall consciously what we see and hear or what happens to us. I don't always remember the television show or movie I watched the night before.

I think in some ways I was more prepared than many. I've had out-of-body experiences that are similar to NDEs. My understanding is that when we completely vacate the body—or "die"—we undergo a series of detachments to finalize the procedure. However, in out-of-body experiences the silver cord remains intact—we are still connected to the body while consciousness is out exploring.

In the summer of 1984 I had gone to sleep and John was sitting up in bed reading. Suddenly, out of the corner of his eye, he saw me leave my body, float across him, and exit through the wall of our bedroom. When he told me about this the next morning, I asked, "What did you do then?" And he said, "What came to mind was that you were getting out ahead of me, so I put the book down, turned off the light, and fell fast asleep. Probably met you out there someplace."

We exit our bodies all the time when we sleep, but mostly don't remember, or else we think of our experience only as a dream. One experience I had was funny, though disconcerting at the time. At a group gathering we'd had a guided relaxation meditation, and after being led into a very peaceful state I was quietly enjoying the tranquillity and felt myself skipping lightly and easily up a staircase. Then I sailed effortlessly in space. I heard the facilitator telling everyone to open their eyes and slowly sit up, so I quickly pulled my attention back to the room. Everyone stood up and so did I, but it felt strange, as if I was out of balance—not really dizzy, but sort of disoriented. Driving home a few minutes later, I began to feel very spacey. Arriving at the house, I wasn't sure what to do, so I took a shower. It didn't ease the disorientation, so I just sat quietly in a chair for a while, and after a time felt myself equilibrate. Later I realized that I had been out-of-body, and when I had jerked myself back in so quickly, I must have come in crooked.

Some people tell me that they can go out-of-body at will and travel to places on this plane and beyond. There have been cases where a person has been seen far from where his or her physical body was located. One of the most remarkable stories of "bilocation" was that of Mary of Jesus of Agreda.

Although she never left her Spanish convent, she was seen ministering to the Jumano Indians of New Mexico more than five hundred times between the years of 1620 and 1631.

In his book *Practical Spirituality* John tells of an interesting adventure he had:

A few years ago I had a bilocation experience where I seemed to be in two places at the same time . . . in my bedroom with Jan, and in a beautiful white temple where I was talking to the old man who appears frequently in my dreams. But this was not a dream. It was very real and I could feel, see, hear and smell with my senses in both locations at the same time.

As I sat across from the man in the temple, I began

to ask questions, and he would answer each question with a question. Staring at me with arms crossed over his heart, he constantly asked, "What do you see?" That's all he ever said in nearly an hour. After a while I could feel myself getting a bit frustrated with the repetition, and it was probably this dissatisfaction with the conversation that suddenly pulled the traveling part of me back into oneness with the other "me" there at home with Jan.

I thought about the experience for the rest of the night, and meditated on it the following day. Several different interpretations came through. [But I felt that the bottom line was that] I was being told to see as Spirit sees—the Reality behind the illusion.[3]

Another question I've been asked is, how did you handle the pain of the heart attack? Obviously not very well; I got out of my body to get away from it! As the pain increased in intensity, I became very still and nonresistant—because conflict increases trauma. I think that people leave their bodies many times to escape pain, although they may appear to be unconscious or in a coma. For example, one of my dearest friends had the experience of a horse falling on him some years back. He recalls looking down and thinking, *I'm okay, but that poor bastard down there has a problem.* Back in the body at the hospital, he discovered that his pelvis was broken.

Another man I know was vacationing in the Bahamas, snorkeling with friends in the clear blue waters, when he saw a boat coming right at him. Knowing it couldn't miss him, he thought, *You're dead, he's going to hit you,* and dove under the water to put some space between himself and the boat. At that point all fear left him, and he found himself watching the scene from a higher level. He remembers being concerned for his wife—she was farther down the beach picking up shells—and hoping she wouldn't see the accident happen. Hearing people yelling, she ran toward them with the shells in her hand. Then he saw his friend who was trying to rescue him almost drown and have to be hauled back to the beach.

The people in the boat finally pulled him in and got him to shore and the hospital. Later, in the hospital, he said to his wife, "You can put the shells down now." She wasn't aware that she was still clutching them in her hand and wondered how he knew. He had seen everything that went on during and after the accident, but had not felt the impact when the boat hit his body and almost severed his leg.

Earlier I mentioned comas. In modern metaphysics a coma—or state of profound unconsciousness—is an escape route arranged by the ego to avoid facing the third-dimensional consequences of an accident or illness. It is a way of avoiding the fear relating to responsibilities incurred. In ageless wisdom we learn that a coma is a way of working with the Law of Liberation (the death process), and the surrender and willingness to die can pull the individual into deep unconsciousness as a preparatory stage for the soul's withdrawal.

There is also the "coma of restoration," in which personal consciousness is withdrawn to give the Higher Nature the opportunity to restore the body to health without conflict.

There have been many stories of people appearing to loved ones as they make their exit from this life. I remember reading years ago about the famous Arthur Godfrey being visited briefly by his father while on a ship in the Pacific during World War II. Shortly after the experience, a telegram arrived telling of his father's death.

In October 1989 a friend invited us to his lovely ranch for dinner along with visitors from out of town. After a delicious meal, enhanced by stimulating conversation, he suggested that we have a silent meditation together. After a few moments I felt very relaxed and peaceful. Then I felt a large energy form, rather heavy, hover around me. It seemed to want to speak. Though it didn't feel negative in any way, I didn't feel comfortable about it. The only words I heard were "Be still, little one." Then it went away. The next morning we learned that Jeanie, John's stepsister in California, had died the night before—at the precise time we were having the meditation. I believe she stopped to say good-bye.

10

Cracks in the Veil

Near-death experiences have been reported for centuries, which helps us to understand that the opening between the earth plane and beyond was never permanently sealed; there have always been cracks in the veil. In referring specifically to ancient times, Manly Hall writes, "Men have died and have lived again; for returning from the vale of shadows, they have described, with minute detail, that which they experienced and beheld."[1]

In his book *The Phoenix*, Hall reports on the death and return of Cleonymus, an ancient Greek.

After he was laid out and prepared for burial, a gentle breathing was perceived and interment was halted. Cleonymus, after a short time, was restored to physical vigor and described in detail what he had seen and heard while his soul was absent from his body.

He related how his soul, or rational part, was as

though liberated from bondage so that it soared up from body and, having ascended above the earth, came into places of "various figures and colors," with rivers unknown to man. Still ascending, he came to a region sacred to Vesta and was brought into the presence of gods of indescribable forms. His narrative reminds one of the world described by Socrates in his last discourse—an aerial sphere wherein beings dwelt along the shores of the atmosphere even as men dwell along the shores of the sea. The story of Cleonymus is vouched for by Clearchus, who was a disciple of Aristotle.[2]

Another example from the ancient past is that of Polycritus, a prominent citizen among the Ætolians. "Polycritus returned to life after being dead for nine months. . . . After returning from his wandering in fourth dimensional vistas, Polycritus seemed to have increased in wisdom to a marked degree, from which it was evident that he had found favor with the gods."[3]

From Socrates to Cicero before Christ, from Plutarch to Swedenborg *Anno Domini*, there are numerous reports of people who have died and were called back "to bear witness to the superphysical mysteries of life."[4] But nothing can compare with the extraordinary number of near-death experiences that have been recorded in the twentieth century—and the past twenty years in particular. Death and return has become almost commonplace.

What has this well-beaten path of comings-and-goings done to that energy vortex within each one of us that represents the door, or veil, between the two worlds? Has the collective density been reduced to such an extent that it is no longer a substantial barrier? In my opinion the answer is yes. I believe that there is now a permanent rip in the curtain, enabling those on the other side to enter the physical world at will. Though the projection into this plane from the other side may last only a short time, there is evidence that visitations are now occurring with greater frequency than ever before.

In March 1940 Mrs. Ruth Whittsley was living with her husband, a minister, in Hawthorne, California. Mrs. Whittsley was superintendent of a small convalescent hospital. On this particular occasion she was called because a patient was dying. She told her husband she had to go to the hospital, hurriedly dressed in her nurse's uniform, and started out. It was the middle of the night.

Mrs. Whittsley found that her car would not start. She considered calling a cab, then decided, since the hospital was only two blocks away, to walk.

The adjoining block was lonely, with no houses or streetlights. As Mrs. Whittsley left the lighted area, a small car with two men in it emerged from the darkness and pulled up beside her. She started to walk faster, then to run, but the car followed slowly, a few feet behind her.

Suddenly Mrs. Whittsley saw a warmly familiar sight. Her big white collie, Nigel, raced up and planted himself between her and the car. She noticed one of the men lean out and look at the huge dog, then the vehicle roared off into the darkness.

The dog stayed with Mrs. Whittsley until she reached the next streetlight, which was only a stone's throw from the hospital. Then the white collie was gone. Mrs. Whittsley reached the hospital still in a state of near shock. As several nurses gathered around asking what was wrong, she started to recount her frightening experience with the car, the two men, and her collie, Nigel.

Suddenly Mrs. Whittsley stopped in midsentence. Her face grew even paler. For a moment she looked as if she might faint. Her faithful dog, Nigel, had died *six months before*.[5]

After my return trip, our dog, Maggi, visited us several times. First she was in my meditation chair the morning after I came home from the hospital, and though I couldn't see her, I could feel her body next to mine as she gave me a big slurpy kiss on the face. We also felt her in our bed several times, and one evening John saw her walking in front of him in the backyard, moving her body in her distinctive, segmented tootsie-roll walk.

People who have had a near-death experience often find they can communicate with the other side, and at times have visual contact. I met one woman who commented that she had more "dead" visitors in her home than those who were in physical form. Jean, whose NDE I shared earlier, found this to be true. While sitting with her dying husband she saw his deceased father appear beside his bed. The father told her he had come to get his son.

A woman I met in Missouri wrote about a visit from her mother. She said,

As I lay crosswise in the bed, I felt it sink in beside me. I could feel the presence of someone and I opened my eyes. It was my mother who had passed away in 1951. She and I were so very close. I sat up and we embraced, our arms closing about each other.

As she held me, I looked over her shoulder, and she said, "What do you see behind me?" I could see grand-mother, grandfather, my husband's late sister, and quite a few others who I knew had passed away, and I said this to my mother.

"What are they doing?" she asked.

I told her that they were waving and smiling. They looked radiantly healthy, and in the distance I could see them in a brilliantly lit area, and the colors were very bright. I knew in my heart that they were alive.

Mother said, "There is no death, only different states of beingness; at a certain point in time we step out of one suit of clothing, so to speak, and into another."

These words really reached my heart and I knew she was right. We spoke for a short time, then she blessed me and gave me her love, and then disappeared.[6]

A friend of ours, Enid, shared a fascinating story with us, which John included in his book ANGEL EN-

ERGY: *How to Harness the Power of Angels in Your Everyday Life*. She wrote in part,

> "Shortly after my mother made her transition, I was meditating with my prayer group. I felt a sense of completion with the meditation, and was waiting for the others to stir. Suddenly before me was a shimmering, vibrating cloudlike essence of lavender, pink and silvery light. It floated in a wavelike manner before my eyes and was sort of upright in form, tapering near the bottom."

A friend sitting next to Enid told her later that the image she had seen was that of her mother: " 'She went on to tell me that my mother was there with us and had given her a message for me. The personal message was such that I knew no one could have given it but my own mother.' "[7]

Although we didn't realize it at the time, John and I were part of a strange and wonderful event in December 1988. It happened at that dusky time of day just before the night falls completely. I was in the kitchen when the doorbell rang, and wondered who it might be, as no one was expected. When I opened the door, I saw a young man, probably nineteen or twenty years old. He had a gentle, sweet face, and I perceived there to be a glow about him even though the outside lights were not on yet.

He asked if a certain family lived here, the former

owners of the house, but I told him that they had moved to San Antonio. He said he had been away for a while—that he had known their sons—but that he really wanted to talk to "Mr. Jones" and to thank him. He explained that some years before, his father had lost his job and could not find work anywhere, and that just when they were about to lose all hope, Mr. Jones found a job for the father and saved the family.

I offered to give him Mr. Jones's address and phone number, but he said he couldn't stay long. I said, "What is your name? I'll tell them you came by."

He said, "Toddy," then thanked me and turned and walked down the driveway.

John and Maggi had walked up while we were talking, and listened to the conversation. Oddly, Maggi didn't bark as usual when someone came to the door. As we went back inside, John asked, "Did you see a car?"

"No. He must have parked out on the road, but I didn't hear a motor start up."

Some months later "Mr. Jones" came out to show us how some of the equipment on the property worked, and we told him about the visitor who had come to thank him. At first he didn't recognize what the young man had been talking about, but after a moment he said, "I do recall something; there was one situation like that. Do you remember his name?"

"Toddy," I replied.

"I don't want to hear this," Mr. Jones shouted. "Are you trying to spook me?" He began to walk back toward his car, then paused and turned around to face us. He said, "Toddy was killed two years ago on an oil rig in south Texas."

It was obvious he didn't want to discuss it further, and the conversation ended at that point. We've never forgotten the experience, nor the look on the man's face when we told him about the visitor.

Some things cannot be explained; they just have to be accepted. Isn't it beautiful to know how thin is the veil between worlds? So thin that a young man with love and gratitude can somehow move through it to deliver belated heartfelt thanks to a benefactor.

John's father died when he was eleven, but has appeared several times when his mother needed assistance. One occasion was rather humorous. She had left the water hose on one night when she went to bed, and during the night the water pressure increased tremendously. Awakened by the phone ringing, Mom sat up in bed and picked up the receiver. Her husband's familiar voice said, "Eva, you'd better turn off the sprinkler; water is spewing like a geyser." She rushed outside to turn off the water, and when she turned around, he was standing in the picture window laughing.

At another more serious time, when her second husband was hospitalized due to a stroke, he came again. Since it appeared there would be a lengthy recovery, Mom was looking for a place near the hospital to stay. Walking down the street, he appeared beside her to give her loving support—and directions to a suitable apartment.

Mom also tells about the experience when he was

dying and family and friends were gathered around the bed. Suddenly he exclaimed, "Why, there's Ora." His sister who had died many years before had come to greet him.

The April 1994 issue of *Guideposts* reflected on the life of Norman Vincent Peale, and one article told of him receiving the news of his mother's death and putting his hand on a Bible on the desk. As he did so, he felt a pair of hands touch his head "gently, lovingly, unmistakably." He believed it was not an illusion or a hallucination, but his mother reaching across the "gulf of death to touch and reassure me."[8]

Dr. Peale also tells of an experience when he was speaking at a church convocation in Georgia. At the close of the service all the ministers present were asked to come to the front and sing. "Watching them come down the aisles, I suddenly saw my father among them," he wrote. "I saw him as plainly as when he was alive. He seemed about 40, vital and handsome, singing with the others. When he smiled at me and put up his hand in an old familiar gesture, for several unforgettable seconds it was as if my father and I were alone in that big auditorium. Then he was gone. But he was there, and I know that someday, somewhere I'll meet him again."

In another story he tells about his father appearing to his stepmother in a dream and saying, "Don't ever worry about dying. There's nothing to it." What was so special was that phrase was something they had heard him use many times.

Another experience shows us that the love connection is so strong that communication can occur over great distances as well as from one plane of existence to another.

In 1980 Laura and a friend were traveling from Denver back to Texas when she had an urge to call home—home being Atlanta, Georgia, where she was raised and her parents still lived. They pulled up to a restaurant outside of Denver and went in. While waiting to be seated, she saw a woman get up and walk to the cash register to pay her bill. It was her mother.

I felt faint, and then thought twice and realized that it could not be her; besides, this woman was happy and younger-looking. As we were escorted to our seat, I overheard the cashier ask the woman if she was ready to leave. The woman said in a voice that sounded just like Mom's, "Not yet, but soon."

I sat down and turned to look at her again, but she was gone. Again I had a strong urge to call home, but let it pass because I knew that now would probably not be a good time. My move to Texas had upset my mother very much, and calls home were usually not pleasant.

We finished our coffee and continued our journey. I thought about that woman and what she had said about not being ready to leave. I knew my mom and how she had expressed often that she did not want to live anymore, but she had a great fear of dying and chose to stay instead.

Arriving home after a twenty-three-hour drive, we

were exhausted. As our heads hit the pillow, the phone rang. It was my sister telling me that Mother was in the hospital. She'd had a severe asthma attack and they thought they had lost her, but she was stable now. I knew immediately that she had died and had come back at the exact time I saw the woman in the coffee shop. My sister confirmed the time, and chills ran up and down my back.

Mother seemed to be recovering well, so I decided to wait until her birthday to go home. Things got sort of weird, though. Mother started contacting relatives she had not spoken to in years. She also wrote me a long letter expressing her understanding of me leaving home. She hoped I was happy and was very proud of my independence. This was a great relief to me, for I had never meant to hurt her.

I was learning to do stained glass and decided to make Mom a rose window for her birthday. Because of her allergies, I had never been able to give her fresh flowers as a child, and I knew how much she loved roses. But two days before I was to leave for Georgia, Dad called and told me she had passed away. Needless to say, I was crushed. I packed my bags and the stained-glass rose and headed home.

I arrived home to a house that still looked as if I had left the day before. Dad was quiet, but strong and practical as always. We went to the funeral home, and as friends of my mother would come up to me, I heard my mother tell me things to say to them. Relatives I had never met would approach, and I heard her tell me their names. I felt her presence so strongly and wondered if others could feel it too.

We went home that evening and went to bed. At three A.M. I got up and went into the living room. The light was on and Mom's rocking chair was moving. This shook me up some, and I sat down to get a grip. Looking up again, I saw her sitting in her chair holding the stained-glass rose. She said, "Thank you. I love you. I'm at peace now." I started to go get Dad, but she was gone.

I saw Mother often for the next two years. She would sit on my bed at night and talk to me, give me advice, or just a pat on the back. When I became pregnant, she told me she would be with me until the baby was born, telling me things I needed to do to prepare for the birth. Sure enough, since the child was born, I have not seen or heard her again.

At one time Laura worked at the ranch conference center where we had our office and held seminars. Beth and her husband Jim lived and worked on the ranch, and were dear to all of us. Shortly after Beth died, Laura walked out of the kitchen one morning and saw Beth coming toward her with a big smile. Later she told Jim, and he said, "Did you really see her?" Laura replied, "Yeah, I did, and it seemed so natural that at first I didn't remember she had died." Jim said, "I saw her yesterday. She's just saying her good-byes."

My friend Betty, whom I've known since childhood, shared the remarkable story of her mother's passing.

Mrs. Smith had suffered a stroke and could no longer speak, but she could still communicate with those beautifully expressive eyes I remember so well. Betty and her daughters are fortunate to have eyes like that too.

The family knew Mrs. Smith was in the death process, and on the night before she died, Betty was sitting with her in the hospital and noticed she was staring at the corner of the room, as though watching something or someone. Betty asked her mother if she saw Smitty, who had been her husband. Mrs. Smith flashed those eyes quickly toward her, as if to say, "How did you know that?"

Betty said, "I've heard that loved ones come for us when we die, and have always believed it so. It's all right for you to go, Mother. We'll be okay."

Her mother's eyes softened and her eyes seemed to smile.

When my friend woke the next morning, something told her to get to the hospital quickly. One of her daughters went with her, and when they entered the room and heard the labored breathing, they knew it was almost over. The nurse who had so lovingly cared for Mrs. Smith suggested they all join hands and sing together to send her on her way.

Standing around her bed, they sang the words of an old gospel song called "Coming Home." As she let out her last breath, Betty noticed that the body seemed to deflate, and then she saw a vaporish shape move upward and go out the corner of the room. After that she knew she could never have any fear of death.

11

Memories
and Understanding

From time to time magazines feature makeovers showing before and after shots. The difference is often remarkable, and the subject is so happy with the results that they feel like a new person. After my other-world tour a number of people commented on how great I looked—younger and prettier—and I definitely felt different than I had before. Now, I'm not recommending that great health spa in the sky for a makeover, but I do feel that the before and after analogy is an excellent way to look at the near-death experience.

The "before" is the period of preparation that each one of us must go through prior to death. How we live on earth prepares us for the other side—it's the first half of the makeover. The "after" is life beyond the veil and what we experience in that other world. If the magnetic thread or silver cord is not broken, we return to the physical plane and death is reinterpreted as "near-death"—the only difference being that we "lived" to tell, or write, about what we experienced.

There are books, I've discovered, that tell us how to prepare for our imminent death. While I'm sure they are worthwhile and can give us much information, I believe the formula I've been given is the ultimate procedure to prepare for the moment of our transition. It is: *Look not to death, but to life for the instruction.* How well we live denotes how we will die and what we will experience in the hereafter.

The Life Instruction Manual comes with a super-duper teacher, Maestro Cause and Effect. This impersonal, nonjudgmental law will play whatever tune we request, and if we don't like it, we can choose another. Knowing we can do that is important; otherwise we could stay stuck in a slow, solemn, mournful funeral dirge.

The creative energy of the universe is amenable to our dictates, and we mold it with the direction of our thought. The idea that what goes around comes around—that we reap what we sow—is right on. That golden rule, which is stated in some way in all religions, is good advice: Do unto others as you would have them do unto you. Even more, keep your mind stayed on that which you wish to experience; don't wander off into the soap operas going on around you, for you might get a role in one of them.

Look at the words of Paul, once known as Saul of Tarsus. Cranky as he was about some things, his wise words in Philippians 4:8 should be our guide: "What-

soever things are true, whatsoever things are honest, whatsoever things are just, whatsoever things are
pure, whatsoever things are lovely, whatsoever things
are of good report; if there be any virtue, and if there be
any praise, think on these things."

And if we don't? Fortunately, as we go through physical life, we find numerous opportunities to balance the
ledger—to right a wrong, correct our mistakes, and
mend our fences. I went across with some pockets of
guilt, but because I was coming back, I had the chance
to empty them out. What if I had stayed? Would I have
had access to the various planes? In time yes, because of
the spiritual work that I've done over the years. But I
would still have had to clean up my emotional nature
before proceeding to the higher realms. Since I like direct flights with no stopovers, I want to make sure that
next time I'll slip through those gates with the highest
state of consciousness possible. You want that, too, so
maybe my looking back at the "before" stage will help
you take a closer look at yourself.

Living on the earth plane is a time to grow emotionally, mentally, and spiritually. I know I have, and in the
process I've changed and modified many of my beliefs.
I've learned much by trial and error through interaction
with people, slipping and falling, picking myself back
up again, and reaching and sometimes catching that
shooting star. And sometimes not. That's life. That's
learning, and all the time, consciousness is evolving, re-
vealing more of the truth that's always been there in
the deep recesses of mind.

I think I've always believed in God, and that belief

has made life in the three-dimensional world a lot more pleasant. There was a point somewhere in my teenage years when I began to back away from the religious concepts espoused from the pulpits. I couldn't quite put my finger on the conflict at the time, but something inside me just did not agree with what was being preached. People I met along the way helped reinforce that feeling, and perhaps were responsible for bringing some of that inner knowing to the surface of mind.

Back in the 1950s a friend told me that the Jews were barred from heaven because they didn't believe in Jesus. With her exclusive thinking, she helped me to remember that God is all-inclusive—that every soul is forever a member in good standing in the universal family. A neighbor in the 1960s said that our baby, who had died, was doomed to hell because he had not been baptized. Her comment made me instantly know otherwise. Another friend talked about that so-called literal hell in the great Beyond. This meant there was a punishing God. No way. I couldn't accept that because the "memory" in my mind and the feeling in my heart was only of a benevolent, loving, all-caring God.

My life in physical form could not be called extraordinary from the world's perspective. In fact some would view it as quite ordinary—growing up in a small town, going to college, getting married, working to help with expenses in the early days, having children, playing the role of mother and homemaker, going back to work when the children left the nest. But underlying all of this was something I felt very adamant about—that life is what you make it, that we are the masters of our fate, and that happiness is natural. This belief was reinforced even more when John and I stepped onto the spiritual path.

We were raised Baptists, married in the Methodist Church, and grew much as Congregationists. And then in the late 1960s what we consider our true spiritual journey began. We "remembered" through books, inner guidance, and contacts with illumined people that God, Good, is the only Presence and Power there is, and the only problems we have are those we create ourselves—*by not understanding who and what we are.*

John White, internationally recognized author and educator in the field of parascience and human development, reflects thousands of years of enlightened teaching when he says, *"You are God."* In his book, *A Practical Guide to Death and Dying,* he writes, "This is the core truth of all the world's major sacred traditions. The very essence of all creation—God—is as much within you as it is within trees, mountains, stars and cosmic dust. The condition from which all existence springs—God—is your true identity. When you fully realize the nature of your being, you recognize there is no separation from God and never has been. You are infinite and eternal. You are immortal—not as a separate body or soul in a single permanent state but as that which produces the totality of the universe in all states."[1]

Walking the spiritual path didn't mean that everything was instantly all peaches and cream. There were still problems and challenges to deal with, but a more positive frame of mind helped us move past them with relative ease. Then in 1981 John wrote a book, *The Superbeings*,[2] and our lives changed dramatically. This prompted invitations to discuss our understanding in groups, followed by more books and more opportunities to conduct workshops. During all of this activity we formed the Quartus Foundation for Spiritual Research, which continues to be our communications base.

My philosophy of life echoes the wonderful title character from the Broadway show and movie *Auntie Mame*. At one point she states, "Life is a banquet and most poor suckers are starving to death." Her admonition to all who would listen was, "Live, Live, Live." Among the definitions of the verb *live* in Webster's dictionary is "to have a life rich in experience, to exhibit vigor, gusto, or enthusiasm in, to enjoy a full and varied life." The great wayshower best known as Jesus Christ agreed: "I came that they might have life, and have it more abundantly."

Yes! I believe we should celebrate life by living each day fully—and Emerson did too. The Sage of Concord wrote, "A man contains all that is needful to his government within himself. He is made a law unto himself. All real good or evil that can befall him must be from himself. . . . The purpose of life seems to be to acquaint a man with himself. He is not to live to the future as described to him, but to live to the *real* future by living to the *real* present. The highest revelation is that God is in every man."[3]

Emerson also told us that "Nothing great was ever achieved without enthusiasm"—that "The way of life is wonderful, it is by abandonment."[4] This deeply spiritual man knew how to dispel negative appearances and get to the core of reality: "Exercise the soul, and the weather and the town and your condition in the world all disappear; the world itself loses its solidity, nothing remains but the soul and the Divine Presence in which it lives."[5]

To find joy in life, he said we should "fill the hour,— that is happiness; to fill the hour and leave no crevices for a repentance or an approval."[6] And his view of *living* was that "All life is an experiment. The more experiments you make the better. What if they are a little coarse, and you may get your coat soiled or torn? What if you do fail, and get fairly rolled in the dirt once or twice? Up again you shall never be so afraid of a tumble."[7]

In our time, author and health consultant Susan Smith Jones, Ph.D., writes, "To live fully means living passionately, peacefully, joyfully, and healthfully while celebrating and playing at this game of life. In order to do this, look at your life from a higher perspective rather than getting caught up in the day-to-day inconsequential matters. Love all aspects of your life. Be grateful for your challenges for they make you grow and become stronger."[8]

As I was writing this chapter, I remembered a priceless gift from one of my daughters, something that lays out my philosophy of life in better words than mine. In a double frame is a picture of us together on one side, with a message on the other, titled, "Things My Mother Taught Me." It reads: "How many little girls went looking for fairies in the woods with their mother? Or were awakened by Mom pulling a kitten out of her robe pocket? Or had their toast cut with cookie cutters? I did. My mother shared a wonderful philosophy with me—'Life is fun. Enjoy it!' "

Perhaps from this you'll have some idea of the attitude and feelings that I took with me on my trip beyond the veil. And what I found on the other side was indeed paradise—not so much because my consciousness was in the "seventh heaven" category, but for the reason that I believed in the eternal love and goodness of God, that the Spirit of God was within me, as the Reality of me, and that life was meant to be enjoyed in all its fullness. This was my preparation for the journey.

The second period of our discussion—the "after" stage—began with the awareness that I was completely content to be where I was at the time—on another plane of existence. I felt no sadness or fear, no emotions about having left the physical world and no desire to come back. Later, when I knew I was going to return, that was all right too.

I say again that there is nothing to fear about death. Most fear centers around the loss of the body, but I can tell you that the only body we lose is the one made for earth, not the real one, with which we cross over.

When the vital signs cease, we simply move up and out of the fleshly vehicle, and we're on our way. I didn't have to think about how to get out—the soul takes care of that in a perfectly normal and natural process.

I used to wonder if everything on the other side would be spectral, eerie, phantomlike. It's not. Entering that realm, I found a beautiful new environment—a substantial reality. I say "substantial" because there was firmness in form, a feeling of solid substance—whether with people, animals, the "ground" on which I walked, nature in all its glory, or the great variety of structures. So life continues in surroundings that are not foreign to the human condition; there's no shock to the system.

And as I've said, this new life is also an extension of where we were in consciousness. To borrow the title of Tom Johnson's book to make a point, You Are *Always* Your Own Experience—"the identity that you live is the identity that you experience,"[9] regardless of the plane of life. Again we see the necessity of right preparation.

I discovered the other side of death was a most interesting place to be, and I was fascinated at how quickly knowledge came into my mind. Of course, as with all of us, enlightenment had been in the deeper recesses of consciousness all the time, but screened out by an intense focus on the frantic physical world about me. Over there, without every sight and sound competing for attention, it was easy to be attuned to Universal Mind, of which we are eternally one regardless of the plane of life. I didn't have to try to understand. Before a question formed in my mind, I had the answer. That capacity stayed with me to some extent when I returned. Now, instead of trying to figure something out, I simply still my thoughts and a gentle knowing enters my mind.

Another by-product of the NDE is increased intuition. I will suddenly have knowledge or understanding about a person or situation without mentally trying to obtain the information. When this occurs I have complete, unquestioning trust that it is so.

I've been asked what I learned about "religion." For one thing, there is not an angry God, a literal hell, or a valley of sorrows where we are punished for our sins. Man-made religion came up with this idea, and it is a false one. Further, my experience has shown me that whatever our "religion" is—what we devoutly believed in—is what we'll find. The Jew will find Moses, or a Prophet of old. The Christian will see Jesus; the Buddhist, Buddha, and so on. The atheists will find that life continues—that the man-made God they rejected truly does not exist—but that there is a universal Presence and Power that is the life in all things. Most often of high intellect, they will eagerly partake of the opportunities afforded to study and learn the workings of the cosmos. As with all of us, greater understanding will come.

I also came back from my visit knowing that the "theology" of heaven is universal; we can never be separate from God; we are our own devils; there is no original sin; every soul is an incarnation of God; and a critical, condemning, judgmental person, or an extremely fearful one, will find that state of consciousness externalized on the other side. Like Job, that which we feared has come upon us. Deeply embedded religious concepts based on fear may also outpicture, which helps us to see why some near-deathers report some not-so-heavenly experiences. It wasn't hell, only the person's consciousness showing itself.

Is there a reuniting of families? Only if there is a love connection. "Family" in its truest sense is only a group of people drawn together by consciousness so that the law of cause and effect can be learned in rather dramatic educational experiences. The family is the personality's most difficult training ground, and if two or more people come out of it with love and understanding, the bond will continue on the other side. Otherwise, the relationship becomes one only in recognition and appreciation for the role played.

I've always believed that those who had passed from this plane of existence continued to live in another world—and that included our dog. When she died, my heart broke and I grieved terribly—but when I came back from the other side, the pain of missing her was gone. I had seen her and talked to her, and knew she was strong and well and free. Now I *know* that life continues, and I *know* that at some point in time we can be reunited with those we miss. This deep knowing helps in the grieving process when a loved one goes on before us.

I believe the greatest lesson learned on my journey

into the nonphysical world was the true meaning of love. Love is a word that is bandied about so freely, misused mostly, for we have little understanding of its meaning and power. But that's changing. With each near-death experience, people come back into this world with the understanding that love is the foundation for everything. At an NDE seminar in San Antonio, I heard a man say that the most important thing he learned from the other side was, "All that matters is love and knowledge." I agree, for one opens to the other.

The total emphasis beyond the veil is love, and every teaching over there is based on love. Once in that environment, we know without a shadow of doubt that love is the primal energy that gives life, that creates. A moment in that atmosphere fills us with the understanding that love is free—it can't be bought—that love doesn't stop loving and perfect love casts out all fear, washing away all pain and grief. We know that "perfect" is a description of love—that love is never imperfect or it is not love, and that if fear is present, love is not absent but simply unrecognized.

One step into the light beyond and we realize that love is synonymous with that which we call God. And upon returning to this world, love forever has a new meaning—and we know we can never be separated from the source and substance of all that is.

Every man's life is a fairy tale,
written by God's fingers.
—*Hans Christian Anderson (1805–1875),
Danish author*

12

Bless Your Heart

The memories and understanding gained from my near-death experience would be for naught if I didn't put into practice what I learned. That was brought home to me several times during 1994, particularly when I got caught up in the day-to-day *busy*-ness of this world and temporarily forgot the teachings from the higher realm. Maybe that's why I was supposed to write this book—to have a permanent record of the course of instruction, and to share it with others who have not had the opportunity to travel beyond the veil and return to physical form.

The Ancients taught that nothing ever happens only for the benefit of one person, that what any individual goes through is also a collective experience on some level of the human psyche. In that context, my reminders to play, love, laugh, and live for the joy of it are for you too—that we all may be helped by my visit to the other side.

While in that higher energy we call heaven, I realized the importance of living fully in the present moment while on earth. When I knew I was coming back, a strong urge welled up in me to find greater meaning in the everyday activities of life, to take more time to experience the *now*. That's the natural process on the other side, but on the physical plane our minds become either distressingly scattered in the turbulence of life, or overly focused on our problems.

The man at the NDE seminar I referred to in the previous chapter also told of another instruction given to him about living on the earth plane. It was "Keep it simple." How true!

Several months after my heart attack, I had a little flutter in my chest—probably a twitter to remind me not to complicate things. So I went into meditation and heard a beautifully simple instruction: *Bless your heart*. A smile came over my face and I remembered my childhood: Bless your heart. Bless your heart. Bless your heart, bless your heart, bless your heart. Where I grew up, those words were the standard statement for all occasions.

"Hello, Aunt Fay."

"Well, bless your heart."

"I cut my knee."

"Bless your heart!"

"Mr. Perkins died."

"Bless his heart."

"I won the lottery!"

"Well, bless your heart."

I said it too; still do sometimes. It's good for when you don't know what else to say, and even though it's rote, it could carry some blessings with it. I don't think most people are consciously blessing when they speak it, but they do mean well.

I went back into that secret place within and asked, "How do I bless my heart?"

And I heard, *Fill your heart with love.* Another reminder. It made me think of sweet Flo Green, who told me long ago that she puts love around everything. So I thought I'd put love around my heart and in my heart. What does love look like? Inside I'll put pink stardust to sweeten it, and to cushion it on the outside, I'll put downy white poufs of cloud.

The discomfort was going away.

I remember from Proverbs 23:7, "For as he thinketh in his heart, so *is* he." *Thinketh in his heart.* Yes, the heart center is actually a part of the mental body, so we can bless our hearts by filling them with loving thoughts. "Fill your heart with love," I was told, and we know that love casts out all fear. Where there is no fear, the guilt is gone, and no sentence of pain or sorrow need be inflicted.

I filled my heart with loving thoughts and a week later John and I flew to Ireland for a wonderful vacation. My heart was blessed and so was our trip.

Bless your heart. Let go of any judgment or condemnation of yourself. Stop looking at what is wrong with you. *Nothing* is wrong with you—it's just some misguided creation from the past making an appearance on the screen of life. My near-death experience was a reminder that part of the creative adventure we've undertaken in this dense world of form is to experience what we have set in motion, and to realize unpleasant events may occur, for at some time or another we have thought them up, whether we remember doing so or not.

Bless your heart. Bless it by taking long walks, and not just for the exercise. While in nonphysical form I was awed by the beauty of the world beyond. Why not here, I was reminded. Heaven can be seen anywhere when we look for it. So take long walks to fill your heart with love—and look where you are going. Feel what you see. Let your heart and mind and eyes and feet feast on the beauty and wonders all around you. Think not of how long or how fast you walk. Lose yourself in the joyful experience of movement in this glorious dimension of life.

Bless your heart. Fill it with love by listening. Over there I heard the music of the spheres. There is music here too, everywhere. Be still and hear the rhythm of nature. Sing whatever tune comes into your mind. Sing for the joy of it and listen to yourself sing—and love your song whether it's a cackle or a crystal-clear tone.

Bless your heart. Fill it with love. Whatever the heartache, be it physical or emotional, the healing balm of love will heal, make whole—another reminder from the celestial realm. When I could let it be all right that my heart hurt and take whatever steps were needed to correct the error pattern, I was blessing my heart. If medication is needed, bless your heart by knowing the Godstuff it is. If surgery is needed, bless your heart by allowing loving medical specialists to attend to you. Everything is spiritual when seen from the true perspective—another principle implanted beyond the veil.

Bless your heart by knowing that whatever was set in motion in the past can be changed or erased, because you are omnificent (having all creative power) and can replace fear with love.

Bless your heart. Fill it with love. Talk with the animals; they respond with such love. I spoke with two goats on my walk this morning. I've seen them before, but never stopped to visit. Today they were right by the fence and I could see them up close. A black-and-white one with grayish-colored horns pointing up from his forehead was wearing a smart goatee. The cream-colored female had a soft beard under her chin too, and such sweet doe eyes. They looked up with interest as I made words with my mouth. Though they continued chewing, I felt the radiation of their response to my greeting. Love filled my heart—for them and for myself. Love.

Life—living intelligence—is everywhere, on every plane. I bent down close to the flowers along the way so that I could really see them. Such miracles they are. My heart was filled with love and was blessed by their being—but only because I chose to recognize them could they bless me. The Bible says, "In all thy ways acknowledge him." And my heart sings songs of joyful praise for flowers, trees, birds, and bees.

Bless your heart. Fill it with love. Live life for the joy of it, the delight of it—never for the duty or obligation. That's what I was taught. Whatever happens along the way is part of the adventure—not good or bad, just an experience.

Bless your heart. Fill it with love. Speak words of truth, beauty, and inspiration. My prayer from the Psalms is "Create in me a clean heart, O God, and renew a right spirit within me" (Psalms 51:10). And from Matthew 5:8, "Blessed are the pure in heart, for they shall see God." Yes! Fill your heart with love, and all you will see is God. My experience showed me this.

"For where your treasure is, there will your heart be also" (Matthew 6:21). Fill your heart with love; treasure the love of life. And from Ezekiel 18:31–32, "Cast away from you all your transgressions; and make you a new heart and a new spirit."

Bless your heart. Fill it with love. Listen to the wonderful words of Walter Lanyon:

And I heard the Laughter of God in the Soul of my very being—ringing in glorious cadence throughout my universe, causing me suddenly to burst into a glorious laughter which was full of praise, full of wonder and amazement at that which I had missed through looking through a glass darkly. "Arise, shine; for your light has come" (Isaiah 60:1)—do you hear?

It is wonderful! It is wonderful! It is wonderful! Heaven and earth are full of Thee—sin, sickness, and death have vanished away. I hear the Laughter of God ringing in the deep recesses of your soul, you who read this page. I see the moving finger writing across all the worries and fears of a lifetime "It does not matter," and I see this laughter writing the things of beauty over the walls of your temple and casting a glorious glistening white robe—a seamless robe of attainment—over you. And at last I hear you laughing from the mountain peak as you go on your way.[1]

Listen for that laughter now. I hear it, and also the words from my time in the rarified energies of that other land ... *Happiness is holy!*

13

The Beloved
Old Friends

Earlier I reported on the Master Teacher in the
temple who told me that much knowledge would
be brought into remembrance bit by bit after I returned
to the body. Then he said, *"Beloved old friends will continue to work with you, as we have in the past."* And,
"Yes, I am one of them."

As we have in the past . . . . I am one of them. This was
a revelation for me, because I had not known that the
teachings I received a few years ago were from this level
of wisdom. Did I go there in some form of out-of-body
experience, or did they come to me through a crack in
the veil?

I understand now that these teachers continually
send forth their loving intelligence *through* the veil,
hoping these seed thoughts will find fertile minds operating on a higher frequency. And they are. Individuals
around the world are accepting new ideas coming to
them "in a flash," or as a gentle dawning in conscious-

ness. And as they contemplate this wisdom, their belief system changes and they approach "the realm of truth" so often discussed in the philosophical circles of the distant past. This is what happened to me more than three years ago, and the experience brought me into conscious communication with a higher realm.

I have long known that there is another reality right where we are, another world, and I have tapped into it and even visited there at times. Emerson called it the Mid-World—"the equator of life, of thought, of spirit, of poetry—a narrow belt."[1] We live there too, and that part of our self is ever drawing our awareness back to it. Multidimensional beings we are, existing simultaneously on different levels of consciousness. As we begin to contemplate the idea that there is more than what appears through our physical senses, strange and wonderful events begin to occur.

John agrees with this, and wrote an article for *The Quartus Report* about it. "I now believe that each individual on this planet is a multi-dimensional being— an electromagnetic field of conscious energy extending, simultaneously, back in time and forward into the *now* of multiple worlds," he wrote. "We are stretched out in spacetime, and the particular 'world' that we consider our primary reality is where the preponderance of our conscious awareness is focused at any given moment. We are where we are in mind and feelings."[2]

Vitvan, founder of the School of the Natural Order, calls these other realities "higher frequencies." He says,

We live in an "ocean" of energy-frequencies. Our awareness of these frequencies depends upon our ability to register them. This ability we can develop as certainly as we can tune in on vibrations or radio frequencies with a radio. Receptivity counts heavily here: what we get depends, in one instance, on the radio, and in the other, on one's state of awareness. . . .

The energy waves and frequencies are reality. All pure knowledge comes from registering the higher frequencies of the Noetic level; that is what is meant by "contacting the Source"; and there is nothing vague or dreamy about the procedure. It is definite.

You can know more and more in only one way: by developing the ability to arrest relatively higher energy wave-lengths and frequencies in this illimitable ocean of energy-wave-lengths and frequencies in which you live, move, have your existence and Be-ing.[3]

In November 1991, during my morning prayer and meditation time, I had a very unusual experience. I had written in my journal, "Today I am at peace, within-without, is peace." Then into my mind came the word *Illuminati*, and the inner knowing that I was in the company of illumined ones. All around me I felt their presence—willing teachers, ready to inspire—and their knowingness flowed into me.

With their help I was lifted to another level of being—a higher frequency—a place of quiet beauty and gentle, loving companions. I saw a summer porch, tree branches, people sharing, and I recognized them. They were friends, beloved old friends. And they shared that they were working with me on that level to draw me back to the fullness of that mind.

I was told, *"Teach to remember what is known. The veil is thin and can be penetrated. Each must learn to receive information from Self. We assist you to align your vibration to your own lifestream or current. We stand with your Self multiplying and amplifying the energy to pull you into knowingness. You will work there with full knowledge as you are aware and integrated with Self here. All ideas have completeness flowing behind them. As you open more, you will not think separately."*

They are there for all of us. If we desire it enough, they will blend their energy with that of our very own Self to amplify it, multiply it, and draw us in to that level of energy.

It was the first of many such meetings. I was told not to concern myself with writing all the details, but to experience what they were sharing—that more would come, to practice tuning in. They can be with me without it affecting what they normally do, and say that some who see them think of them as angels. I felt grateful and excited, and thought, *I have friends in high places!*

Another time when I was in that higher frequency, balls of energy were shooting back and forth between "my friends"—like a game of catch with no bodily movement. It was as though they were projecting the energy with their minds. They were having a wonderful time, and said that I could do it too. *"Just gather the golden light up in your mind, shape it and project it. Aim it where you wish and see it go. When it hits, it scatters into a thousand bits like a starburst. Send it where you will; it is pure love in its natural state.*" I sent it to them, and they sent it back to me, and at a certain point I felt that a whole vat of love-light had just been poured on me. They laughed at my response.

Though it is a delightful game, working with the energy in this manner is not child's play. That starburst of the primal energy of love, which contains peace, joy, and other beautiful attributes, goes in and makes an impression. We don't tell the energy what to do; love knows what is needed and is ever giving of itself to reveal perfection. We can direct it to a particular person or place, or just send it out into the world to do its healing work.

At times I felt rhythmic vibrations up and down my body, pulsating in certain areas. When I asked what it was for, I was told that it was *"energy stimulation to raise the vibratory level so that we can communicate better."* Then in answer to my unasked question came the message that they do not interfere with me—that they only help to activate the awareness of Self. Our Source is the same, and they magnify my own Light, intensifying my awareness of higher mind.

In *Seat of the Soul* Gary Zukav writes, "Long before we, as a species, became aware that there is such a dimension as the realm of nonphysical guidance and Teachers, each human was guided, and beautifully, by many nonphysical teachers."[4]

Zukav also says, "A nonphysical teacher brings you ever closer to your soul. It draws your attention to the vertical path, and to the difference between the vertical path and the horizontal path.

"The vertical path is the path of awareness. It is the path of consciousness and conscious choice. The person who chooses to advance his or her spiritual growth, to cultivate awareness of his or her higher self, is on the vertical path."[5]

The next communication came from a different energy coordinate. Conversations with the friends seemed to come from around me, this from directly above. Such love I felt, a joining, like being woven in a tapestry of love. *"The love you feel is my love too . . . the love for myself which is you. I am that part of you that lives on a higher level, and I am loving you back. Feel, feel . . . this love is for you, of you."* I felt a dancing movement inside, and an awareness of being filled. It was as though there was more of me than there had been before.

As time went on, I looked forward with great anticipation to these visits. The whole purpose, I knew, was to bring me into greater awareness of my spiritual nature, that beautiful spirit of Jan that is connected to the energy of All That Is—to open my human thinkerpart to that vast library of mind that is ever available to all of us through our Higher Nature. As I focused my attention more and more on that beam or ray that extends from where I sit in physical form to the body of light, then to that point of light from which all emanates, I saw the interconnectedness of myself, everyone, everything, within that great being we call God.

I completely understood the great commandment to love the Lord thy God with all thy heart, soul, mind, and strength—and to love thy neighbor as thyself. The only way we can love our neighbor is to love ourself, for our neighbor is ourself, and the only way we can love ourself is to love the Lord our God, for we are one.

In his book *Empowerment* John wrote,

How do we bring in that Higher Mind to dramatically transform our world? By meditating on the Great Self within, which connects us with the Gaze and fills our heart center with the Truth that sets us free. . . . Think of the heart as a circle of light that expands with every degree of Self recognition, ever enlarging to accommodate more and more of the Divine Incarnation.

From the Blazing Sun of Love within, the all-inclusive Rays shine forth to express the Unlimited All-Good. It is our Self fulfilling Itself through us, and consciousness is the acceptor, the transformer, and yes, the Limiter. . . . But we will not be open to that Love and cannot reverse the laws of mental and emotional gravity until we take the necessary steps in this world to clean up our mess. This was spelled out very clearly in John 5:17—"My Father is working still, and I am working." It must be a cooperative effort of conscious mind and Master Self working together. Through our attunement with Self, we can be guided every step of the way.[6]

We are so much more than we see in the mirror. To help illustrate this, I want to share part of a letter from a dear lady I correspond with in California. In a meditative experience she had a vision, and as she tells it, "I felt myself to be 'up' somewhere in what I can only call 'the stratosphere.' I felt myself to be infinite, without form, a sort of light radiating out in all directions. Looking down, far down, I saw my physical self as a tiny doll-like figure in a meditative pose. Though I used the terms 'up' and 'down,' there was no separation. The tiny form below seemed remote, yet somehow connected. And I thought, 'Down there is a tiny aspect of myself, but my Self is here.' Then I thought of the 91st Psalm, and that I AM 'in the secret place of the Most High' *NOW!*"

Recently I observed with my inner vision a face smiling down on me. On my morning walk I was thinking of this, and words began to form a song—"There's a face I see smiling down on me, Shining down on me such joviality." Joviality, of course, relates to Jove, which used to be a term for deity or God, which made me think of Henry Higgins's line in *My Fair Lady*, "By Jove, I think she's got it." Then I remembered reading that Emerson said he was often conscious of Jove nodding to Jove from behind our backs—and I got a picture of that in my mind. Yes, there is more of us than meets the eye—the physical eye.

I sat on our deck thinking of what had been revealed to me in recent weeks, and as I looked out toward the hills, the dancing energy outlining the trees caught my eye. I noticed vibrating light surrounding form, seemingly holding it in place, and beyond I saw tiny squiggles filling space.

There is no empty space, I thought, no empty hole, no empty cup. The living substance fills all space, formed and unformed. Where space appears to be is simply unformed energy waiting to be manifest. The form, the vibrating energy field, the substance, and then beyond that, pure golden light. Beyond the solid gold light is more, I know. I'm like the tree; there's more of me. A physical body, and a body of light made from the sparkling substance emanating from the golden light, which comes from beyond.

Not only have I seen the energy outlining the trees off our deck, but once when we lived on Lake Travis outside of Austin, the whole roadside lit up. I was driving along the curvy narrow road, and suddenly the trees, the fence posts, everything, was vibrating light. I pulled off the road to observe this spectacle and realized that everything is alive. There is life, intelligent energy, in all form, or it could not exist. My body is made of the same stuff as the fence post, the flowers, the grass, the river, the earth. If it is intelligent, that means we can communicate with it and learn how to be in harmony with the natural order—the perfect pattern of all that is.

At a conference in Tucson I had a visual confirmation of the power of our words. Between sessions a woman came up to me and began to speak. I could hardly listen to what she was saying because with every word that came out of her mouth, I saw tiny bubbles of energy. There is life in our very words. Those energy bubbles impact the waiting substance, creating form and experience. It would be wise to consider what we are giving birth to with our verbalization, and to practice verbal harmlessness. We should also be very careful what we give life to through our thoughts, and we do this by keeping our minds on the shining radiance.

That smiling face I see shining down on me with such joviality is that part of me that lives on a higher level, the Most High in whose secret place I dwell. "By Jove, I think she's got it!" I am getting it. The more time I spend contemplating the holy presence within, the more complete I feel and the more wonderful ideas and experiences come to me.

You don't have to die to experience ecstasy. You can begin right now!

Life is a quarry, out of which we are to mold
and chisel and complete a character.
—*Johann Wolfgang von Goethe (1749–1832),*
German poet and philosopher

14

Rebirth of the Soul

As we examine the idea of life continuance, the question eventually comes up: Do we ever come back here to earth in physical form? The great majority of the people of the world think so, and this idea certainly makes sense. I learned of the multitude of places of being when I went to the other side of death, and was told none were restricted—the only governor being our state of consciousness. If none are restricted, that would include the place of being we are in right now.

Of course in order to return here, we would have to have a physical body to inhabit. The usual means of doing this is by entering a newborn infant at first breath. That child would have parents and other family members, so we would take on a different identity from the one we had before. You can't do reruns. This is generally referred to as reincarnation.

Lots of people don't like the idea of reincarnation. The first time I heard about it, I was horrified. My ego rose up in revolt against the thought that I had ever had an identity other than the present one. The idea of being in human form as someone other than this distinct personality was completely distasteful, so I rejected it.

Identification with the body and particular personal qualities limits our acceptance of unlimited beingness and is grossly conceited. As we come to understand that we are more than a physical body, more than personality, it is easier to accept that we could have been here before, playing another role. The ego is soothed when it knows that each incarnation is permanently impressed in our individual energy field and never lost.

At a certain point reincarnation begins to make sense. It answers questions about why we have certain tendencies, why some of us are born with birth defects, why we come into particular families, races, and countries. Consciousness outpictures here just as on the other side of the veil, and any unresolved trauma from previous visits establishes a pattern to begin the new embodiment. For example, a spiritual teacher who did great healing work told me the autistic children of today had been shell-shock victims of World War I. Many mysteries can be unlocked with an understanding of where and how they began.

The fact that I had lived many times in physical form was made very clear to me in the Temple of Knowledge. This was not a surprise, for I had been given glimpses of other lives over the years. However, I realize that this concept of past lives is a controversial one, particularly among religionists in Western culture, but a visit to the other side will quickly clear that up.

In line with the thought of ancient civilizations, including the Egyptians, Greeks, and Chinese—and in the religious views of Hinduism and Buddhism—Jesus and the early Christians believed in the concept of reincarnation as a basic "truth." Jesus referred to it in Matthew 11:13–15: "For all the prophets and the law prophesied until John; and if you are willing to accept it, he is Elijah who is to come. He who has ears to hear, let him hear."

In *Here and Hereafter* Ruth Montgomery says that "belief in reincarnation persisted in the early Christian church for several centuries. In the Confessions of St. Augustine 1:6 we read: 'Did I not live in another body, or somewhere else, before entering my mother's womb?' "[1]

Theosophical author Emogene S. Simons says that "Origen, one of the most learned of the Christian fathers, declared, 'Every soul comes into this world strengthened by the victories or awakened by the defeats of its previous lives.' "[2]

When did we stop believing? According to Montgomery,

In the sixth century the Synod of Constantinople (which was not attended by the Pope of Rome) condemned the teaching of reincarnation, and some scholars believe that most references to it were thereupon expunged from the Bible, but among leading Catholic theologians who advocated the philosophy during the Middle Ages were St. Francis of Assisi, founder of the Franciscan Order; the Irish monk, Johannes Scotus Erigena; and the Dominican monk, Thomas Campanella. In more recent times Cardinal Mercier, prelate of Belgium Catholics, stated that the doctrine in no way conflicts with Catholic dogma; and Dean Inge of St. Paul's Cathedral in London declared: "I find the doctrine [of reincarnation] both credible and attractive."[3]

Emogene S. Simons tells us that the doctrine "has been kept alive by individuals ... who have had the mystic vision and the courage to speak their convictions."[4]

According to Simons, people with "vision and courage" would include Ralph Waldo Emerson, Thomas Huxley, Johann Wolfgang von Goethe, Percy Shelley, Arthur Schopenhauer, John Greenleaf Whittier, Walt Whitman, Robert Browning, Alfred Lord Tennyson, Thomas Edison, Henry Ford, and General George Patton. Based on my research, I could add scores of other notables, and in totaling up the numbers worldwide, we see that more people believe in reincarnation than not. Even fundamentalists who believe that reincarnation and the Bible are mutually exclusive regretfully report that "More than 60 percent of Americans consider human events experienced in the past and passed on to future lives to be a reasonable probability."[5]

Why am I including the idea of reincarnation in this

book? Three reasons. First, to emphasize again that once we leave this plane via the death process, we do not become suddenly illumined as Master Teachers. We take our consciousness with us, and continue in the same mind-set and belief system that we had on earth. Second, to show that living in the "heavenly realm" does not mean a fast-forwarding of the evolutionary process into overnight enlightenment. That's simply not the natural process. And the third reason is to show that through reincarnation, we can learn, grow, and eventually return in consciousness to an awakening of our divine nature.

In *Esoteric Psychology I*, we read "All souls incarnate and reincarnate under the Law of Rebirth. Hence each life is not only a recapitulation of life experience, but an assuming of ancient obligations, a recovery of old relations, an opportunity for the paying of old indebtedness, a chance to make restitution and progress, an awakening of deep-seated qualities, the recognition of old friends and enemies, the solution of revolting injustices, and the explanation of that which conditions the man, and makes him what he is. Such is the law which is crying now for universal recognition."[6]

Reincarnation is a recycling program that was never a part of the original intent, or divine plan. It came into being of necessity, and will end when no longer needed. In case you wonder why it started, let me tell you a story:

Bright spirits, God-beings they, were enjoying a romp through the cosmos one day. Noting an area somewhat shrouded from sight, they discovered an as-yet-unexplored space. Intrigued by the dimness, they stopped to observe. Hovering at the outer perimeter, they felt a gentle pulling, rather like a magnetic attraction. Allowing themselves to be drawn in, they were fascinated with the heaviness they felt, and recognized they would need special suiting to explore this new frontier.

Opening their minds to universal knowledge, they perceived how to draw together the substance of which a physical object is composed. With their new bodysuits they were ready to explore and experience this dense level of existence. At first the suits felt heavy and cumbersome, but they soon learned to manage them and thought the whole situation rather a lark. They noticed how solid everything appeared, including themselves, and also found that the body vehicle had strange sensations not altogether unpleasant.

In the beginning we came in and out of this world of matter with ease, simply decomposing the substance forming the body when we chose to leave. Over eons of time we delved deeper and deeper into the dense matter and extended the periods of exploration. As we lengthened the stays in physical form, we became mesmerized by the experiment, and consciousness slowly became opaque. Impervious to the rays of radiant energy because of the sense of separation from Higher Mind, the body began to shut down, and that which we call death began.

Even though these beings exited the bodies that were no longer useful, they could not lift themselves back into that higher plane from which they came. Those still embodied saw the empty shells and thought their comrades no longer existed. They became fearful that it would happen to them too.

Those observing from the higher realms saw what was going on and devised a plan to rescue those trapped in matter, and birth began. It had not been necessary before. This is the second creation, and all of nature reflects it.

As the creative process in generic form began, those who were without body vehicles were drawn into the tiny shapes, giving them life. Before long it was accepted as the natural order of things. Then divisions began—first families, then tribes, towns, nations, races—each protective of its territory and values. Negative thought patterns based on fear and distrust caused disruption of the natural balance, and everything visible began deteriorating. Chaos reigned.

Beings from the higher realm saw that something must be done to penetrate the opacity and, at tremendous sacrifice, began to incarnate in great numbers, hoping to break the spell. Taking with them their awareness of Light, the energy that controls and becomes all form, they became known as Lightbearers. Some were able to retain their awareness in the dense physical and return to the higher realm. Others were trapped like their friends before them—but with a difference. Within them was a remembrance, however obtuse, of the reality behind the illusion.

Through the efforts of the Lightbearers and holy

helpers from the other planes, the consciousness of humanity has begun to clear, and more and more are responding to the great infusion of Light. In time all will remember, and it will be as it was in the beginning.

A fable? Not really. Perhaps not exact in all details, for it happened over a very long time, but true nevertheless.

Nearly everyone has those déjà-vu experiences where you know you've been somewhere before, known someone before, or suddenly know something you have no way of knowing. Of course we've lived before! And some of us remember previous lives—not all the lifetimes, but significant ones that have a correlation with the present one.

In the 1800s I came in twice. The first time I died quite young, only a few years after marrying a man I loved deeply. The discovery of that life came through a piece of poetry I read one day. I knew instantly that it had been written for me, and felt the emotions of that time. Checking it out, I found that the author had written it for his young wife, whose death had left him devastated.

A year and a half later I came back in to be near him, choosing parents who were his close friends. Though we could never be lovers as before, our relationship was extremely close and loving. He encouraged me to write, as I had a flair for it, and I developed quite a successful career with my pen.

There are vivid memories of that particular life because it has direct meaning in my present incarnation. Family obligations were strong, and I felt that I must take care of everyone. I never married, and used my talent to earn money to support the family. As the years went by, the creativity stopped being fun, but I couldn't stop, for someone had to take care of them. Though I loved my family, they were a burden and there was resentment, which caused a great deal of guilt.

I felt restricted in life and thought I'd rather be a man, for they could do things women could not. If you recall, women were rather limited in that era. I also wished for love, but knew it could not be.

There was a love of travel, and twice I went to Europe. On one trip my sister accompanied me and was so taken with France that she returned there to study and eventually fell in love and married. No wonder that my daughter of today so loves that beautiful country and has found a way to live and work there. She was my precious sister in that life.

I remember the last day of that lifetime being spent in a small room—not my home but a place where I was being cared for. It was dimly lit, and there was a little writing desk with yellow flowers in a vase. That was the last thing I saw before dying. Even before I knew this, I've always loved yellow flowers and used yellow daisies for my wedding. I must have died in my sleep, for there was no sensation of discomfort. After death I was in a pleasant place and knew others were nearby. Then I saw the one I now know as John, and we embraced. He was the love in both those lives.

Not long ago John and I bought a new music CD, one that I had not heard before. When one particular selection began to play, I had the strong urge to move my body in a certain way. It was rather like a dance, and I somehow knew there was a reason for each graceful, sensuous movement. Suddenly I was a temple dancer in ancient times, and each movement of the dance was directing healing energy. It was a powerful experience, and made me realize even more that we must develop a greater understanding of the energies and how to use them rightly.

A couple we know told us of their work with past-life regression. He would through gentle suggestions help his wife move into another time and place, then would ask questions, which she willingly answered. One of the lives she told of ended when she was gored by a bull at the age of ten. The event had occurred in the early part of this century in a state not far from where they lived. In researching the material she had given, they first could not locate the town, then found the name had been changed. Further investigation revealed that some of the family still lived there and remembered the incident with the bull. At the old cemetery they visited the grave.

Upon awakening one morning some years ago, I discovered red spots all over my body. This was most distressing, for I did not want to go through life polka-dotted. Sitting down in my meditation chair, I thought, *What is this for?* Immediately I saw myself in medieval times holding a position of power in some type of religious order. Protective of my position, I felt threatened when I observed furtive meetings between the high priest and a beautiful young woman from the village. Spreading rumors about the relationship, I caused the villagers to rise up against her. They dragged her through the streets, then cut her face to mark her as undesirable. She became an outcast and was shunned for the rest of her life. Though I had not expected the action taken, I was responsible and deeply regretted what I had done. The dots? Oh, yes, my death was caused by a pox.

I cried at the horror I'd been shown, and then understood why this remembrance had come to me. In this now-life I was holding back my power to accomplish, to take action, in fear of harming someone. I forgave the "me" I was so long ago, and when I looked in the mirror, the spots were gone.

John has a strong memory of a man and a little boy, both dressed in black, somber-faced, riding in a wagon across a field. Their clothing reflected the Sunday-go-to-meeting type of perhaps the seventeenth century. When we were in Ireland in 1994, he was overcome by melancholy, and the sadness of that memory flooded him. As we talked it over, I asked, "What is in the back of the wagon?" We both immediately knew that it was a casket. All the details aren't clear, but obviously that time was in Ireland, and the man and boy were going to bury a loved one. John was the man.

John also remembers a nineteenth-century lifetime, which for him as for me has great significance for this present one. We are so grateful that this time around we found each other early, and have had many wonderful years together. I was told when I was on the other side, "You've been given everything. Look at your life and be grateful for all you have received." I did, and I am.

In 1984 we were invited to participate in a Valentine gathering and workshop in northern Georgia. Even though we arrived in Atlanta in a blizzard, two delightful people met us and drove us through the beautiful countryside to our destination. The snow gave everything an ethereal appearance, and that set the pace for the weekend. One evening a group of rebirthers came up from Atlanta and we had a group rebirthing session. John and I had not experienced anything like this before and were delighted to have the opportunity. Although I did not tap into any memories, I went to a place that felt so good, I didn't want to come back. Everyone kept calling me and I felt John holding my hand, so I finally reluctantly returned.

John also had an interesting experience. Here's his story:

I was taken back to just minutes before it was time for me to leave the higher plane—the other side—and begin life in this present incarnation as an infant. Jan and I were sitting on a grassy hill, and I was telling her good-bye. The separation of soul mates, regardless the plane of life, can be sorrowful, and as we embraced, a terrible sadness filled my heart. I was leaving first, and even though I knew she wouldn't be far behind—

and that we would find each other again—the parting
was not unlike a predeath scene in our world here. Then
suddenly I was a body of light, and in full
consciousness was hurtling through the tunnel to the
waiting baby.

There's a story in Richard Bach's book *The Bridge Across Forever* that I just love.[7] He and his wife, Leslie, had been studying out-of-body travel and had finally succeeded in doing it consciously. While they were out one night, they noticed a fluffy little light-form and recognized it as their former cat, Amber. As Richard watched, he noticed a silver thread leading down to their present cat, who was asleep on the floor at home. Amber was Angel T. Cat. Yes, cats do it too.

That's not surprising to me, because we now have our dog Maggi back with us in a brand-new body, and this is the fourth time she has been with us that I know of. After meeting her on the other side, I thought she would stay there a while longer. Apparently she decided that John and I couldn't get along without her, because she came back April 28th, and as usual gave instructions in John's dreams on how to find her. This time she brought a friend, and made it clear that he was to live with us too. We call him Casey. It's wonderful to be together again.

Let us live each day well, for it is the foundation for the next day, the next existence, wherever it may be.

> Love is the only thing that we can carry with us
> when we go, and it makes the end so easy.
> —*Louisa May Alcott (1832–1888),*
> *American author*

15

A Spiritual Renaissance

Melvin Morse, a pediatrician in Seattle, has done a great deal of research on near-death experiences among children and whether they produced any lasting effects. In his book *Transformed by the Light* he concludes, "The subject who survives an NDE is irrevocably altered for life."[1] Dr. Morse found that such individuals had almost no fear of death, showed signs of psychic abilities, and usually had a genuine zest for life.

Those I have spoken with are in agreement, and many have become actively involved in service work of some kind. There seems to be an inner direction to move out into the world and help to bring about positive change. Most feel the world is going through a metamorphosis, and like the caterpillar who must let go of the comfort of the cocoon, we must let go of old ways and face change creatively. It is a time of transformation.

More and more people are experiencing near-death,

and the numbers will continue to grow because of new technology, particularly in the medical field. Emergency services such as EMS respond quickly and are trained in various types of resuscitation. Such networks as 911 make it easier for people to get help when needed. And many individuals are taking CPR and other first-aid instruction to be knowledgeable about the appropriate actions to take in emergencies.

Take me as an example. We live in a rural area, but Melody and Carl arrived quickly and had the equipment and knowledge to get my heart started again, and drugs to keep it working on the way to the hospital. Then the sheriff's cooperation through the 911 network cleared traffic for a speedy trip to the soccer field where we met the chopper. Thirty-five miles from the nearest hospital, Airlife got me there in a hurry. A top-notch emergency team was alerted, and going into immediate action made a difference, as did equipment and procedures used by highly skilled doctors. Not many years ago no one would have survived a heart attack such as mine.

That is the exoteric explanation for the increasing number of NDEs, but I believe the *esoteric* one is much more important. And what is this secret and mysterious rationale for all the return trips? It's three-pronged: to help people overcome the fear of death, to provide greater understanding of spiritual phenomena—the *reality* of life—and eventually to turn humanity en masse to the spiritual light.

Think of a map of the United States, or better still the world. Imagine that it is darkened, but each time someone returns from the other world, a light appears in the darkness. Fear has been eliminated in that spot, and greater spiritual understanding comes forth. Such a consciousness is contagious, and the radiance grows, catching others in its light, until at some point the brightness overcomes the darkness completely. Fear of death is no more, and thus begins the elimination of all the maladies that originate with such fear—disease, pain, suffering, and grief. And in the collective mind spiritual reality becomes the core vibration.

"And some great day, all the graves will pop open and the dead will rise up," proclaimed the preacher at my grandmother's funeral. I looked around at the stricken faces of the children and thought about the horror show he had just presented them. No fairy tale, movie, or television show could conjure up a scene as gruesome as that. Not only would we not want to see it, but we sure wouldn't want to *do* it. That would mean that all those people have been just lying there beneath the ground waiting to be called out. No wonder there is a fear of death among so many if they believe they are that body that gets buried.

And maybe it's that particular trend of thought that causes some of the extreme life-sustaining techniques of today, which only prolong the inevitable and deny the dignity of the passage. The fear itself holds many to outdated concepts, and those under its duress may find it harder to accept that a wrathful, judgmental God is actually man's creation.

Perhaps it really isn't dying that is so scary, but what

happens afterward. The scenario above is certainly not pleasant, nor is the idea of hellfire and damnation taught by many religious sects. Teachings that hold fear over the heads of followers deny a God of love and create great anxiety about the qualifications for entrance through their heavenly gate.

The fear of death—and the fear of God—has held mankind in bondage for eons, and the stories we are hearing from so many are lessening that fear. People are bringing back reports of many planes of existence—of nonjudgmental, unconditional love enfolding all creation, of continued opportunities for growth, development, exploration, reunions with loved ones, and more. There are stories of joy, ecstasy, total peace, and utter fulfillment. Men, women, and children throughout the world are learning that death is nothing to be feared, that it's a simple process, like moving from one room to another, without pain or suffering.

The fear of death hastens death by impairing the immune system; freedom from fear builds healthy bodies so that we can live vitally on this plane until our soul issues the call to return home. Death is less complicated with a healthy body—and quicker when the moment is upon us.

But we must not be attracted to death either, nor dedicated to it in our living. "What seems to be the fear of death is really its attraction," says *A Course in Miracles*.[2] The Course also asks, "What would you see without the fear of death? What would you feel and think if death held no attraction for you? Very simply, you would remember your Father, the Creator of life, the Source of everything that lives, the Father of the universe and of the universe of universes, and of everything that lies even beyond them would you remember."[3]

Isn't it amazing what will happen when we no longer fear death? Not only will it be accepted as just a change of locale, but we'll improve physically and remember spiritually. And in this "remembering" we'll find ourselves quite at home with things considered "strange" by fearful folks. This brings us to the second esoteric reason behind all the NDEs: the spread of greater understanding regarding spiritual phenomena.

Reports of what was once considered unusual, abnormal, or "unnatural" are occurring increasingly worldwide. People are fascinated by guidance from inner voices and protection from unseen hands, the many appearances of Mary in different parts of the world, the idea of multidimensional life, mysterious lights, teleportation, the sudden materialization of form out of energy, and other strange happenings. And the appetite for anything angelic is insatiable. You see, what we're bringing back from the other side is the truth that *nothing is impossible, and that things are not what they seem to be on the third-dimensional plane.*

Years ago John and I began to suspect that there was more to this world than what appeared as real to the senses. The first clue was when we were driving to another city—taking a route that was very familiar—and noticed that a small town had somehow vanished. It was a regular coffee stop for us, and according to the road signs and the clock in the car we were there. But it wasn't. Everything else on the drive was normal, and so was the town on our return home the next evening. What had happened? We had risen *above* the town in consciousness. How? Probably through the meditative work that we had done that morning before we left home. Why were we lifted above it? Maybe to avoid an accident or some other negative experience.

Over time we witnessed other unusual happenings— some quite bizarre—and after returning from my NDE I now understand that everyone is really a multidimensional being, an electromagnetic field of conscious energy living simultaneously in multiple worlds. These worlds are within our consciousness and can be found as we rise to higher frequencies in our awareness, which means that our potential to do, be, and have while in physical form is essentially unlimited.

Because of Einstein's work the many-worlds theory is now accepted by many physicists. Each successive world, with its own spacetime and physicality, is a split of the one previous to it—yet there is a slight difference in the vibration of the atomic particles. And the energy becomes finer and brighter until the highest physical realm has been reached—that which has been called "heaven on earth." We know that we do not travel to a particular geographical location to find where one world ends and another begins. The other worlds are dimensional, and can only be reached through portals in consciousness. So the "where" of multiple worlds can only be found in mind.

Emmet Fox, the great metaphysical author and teacher, has written that "Scientific prayer or spiritual treatment is really the lifting of your consciousness above the level where you have met your problem. If you can rise high enough in thought, the problem will solve itself."[4] What he's saying is that when we move, in consciousness, to the next higher level, we are above the problem. It's not where we are anymore—a neat way to solve problems.

Similar to this are the visions shared by Mimi, a Quartus member in California. She is able to move beyond "this world" and connect with all creation and says that these "experiences seem to be a bleed-through or a window opened to a higher dimension. A fog lifted, and I was able to experience life as it truly exists. That world is ever present, but I don't yet have the ability to stay there. These bleed-throughs have served me as near-death experiences have served others. The love that I feel and the more-real-than-real moment in time I experience takes me beyond faith to *knowing* what lies beyond."

The New Physics is studying the reality behind form, that which we call energy, and will develop even further in its discovery and acceptance of new realities. We will rediscover the art of manifestation and of dematerialization. Isolated individuals are doing it now, and have done so all through time. Research authors Louis Pauwels and Jacques Bergier have found that "Newton believed in the existence of a chain of Initiates going back to very early times who knew the secrets of transmutations and the disintegration of matter.

The English atomic scientist, Da Costa Andrade, in a speech delivered at the Newton Tercentenary Celebration at Cambridge in July 1946, made it clear that he thought the discoverer of the laws of gravitation perhaps belonged to this chain and had only revealed to the world a small part of his knowledge."[5]

The "phenomena of multiplication" has been witnessed on so many occasions that several books have been written about it. Sai Baba in India has been the subject of exhaustive studies, and it's been confirmed that he not only manifests objects but also disappears and reappears in another place before one's eyes. When we discover the *natural process* involved in the manifestation of so-called "miraculous provisions," there will be no famine or hunger, for food as well as any other needed commodity will be brought forth from the substratum. Interplanetary travel will be fascinating and educational, and will certainly take care of the overpopulation problem on the planet. Death will be no more, for when we reenact the "Beam me up, Scotty" scene from *Star Trek*, we will know that it works both ways.

Can you get a picture of this way of life? If it sounds farfetched, just think of the changes that have occurred in the last one hundred years. In the 1890s cars were so new and strange that they were shown in circuses. People would have laughed if told that man would soon walk on the moon and that thousands of people would fly across the world daily in a matter of hours. Most plumbing was outside the house, and telephones were barely in existence. There has been a quantum leap, and the leapfrogging continues as each new discovery leads to another.

We will have to get rid of some old ways of thought, just as the idea that the world was flat had to be released. Once that was achieved, ships sailed the seas without the fear of falling off the ends of the earth, and "the new world" was discovered. Of course it had been there all the time, which is what we're finding out about "heaven."

The third rationale for the many near-death experiences is to herald the spiritual renaissance that we've been moving toward for the past century and a half. We are in the midst of it now, and what we are seeing is but a harbinger of what is to come, for there is a growing hunger for something more. A wake-up call is echoing through the cosmos, and there is no shut-off button.

In the 1840s Emerson issued a call for a spiritual revival when he wrote, "America shall introduce a pure religion."[6] And he added, "The foregoing generations behold God and nature face to face; we, through their eyes. Why should not we also enjoy an original relation to the universe? Why should not we have a poetry and philosophy of insight and not of tradition, and a religion by revelation to us, and not the history of theirs?"[7]

In *The Superbeings*, originally published in 1981, John wrote, "Through the silent, hidden work of the Masters, men and women throughout the world are beginning to intuitively understand the Truth. There is a vibration, call it the Master Vibration, that is flowing through the consciousness of mankind, turning each individual toward the Light within, and it is only a matter of time before the Dawning."[8]

And in *The Morning of the Magicians*, written by Pauwels and Bergier and published in 1983, a reference was made to a thirty-year study by geneticist Lewis Terman. The conclusion was that "a superior kind of adult" is coming forward—"gifted with an intelligence that has nothing in common with that of ordinary human beings. They are thirty times as active as a normal man of talent. Their 'success index' is multiplied by twenty-five. Their health is perfect, as well as their sentimental and sexual balance. Finally, they escape the psychosomatic diseases, notably cancer."[9]

What is the catalyst for this pure religion, this Master Vibration, this new person? As I have said emphatically—because it was made very clear to me on the other side—it is *love*. At NDE seminars and symposiums, *love* was the word that was woven through the accounts of those who described their journey into the Beyond. And love is what will pave the way to greater understanding as this dawning New Age is ushered in. Controversial as that term is in some religious circles, it is relevant. We are ever looking to the new age, and there is ever a new age before us.

To apprehend the *agape*, we must contemplate the idea behind the word itself. If love is unconditional, what does that mean? Love itself has no conditions, but also we can put no conditions on love. As we open our minds to know and our hearts to feel this awesome power, it will teach us in its ways.

One night in May 1988 I was awakened and shown faces and scenes of those opportunities to love when I didn't. Subtly and gently I was instructed on love and given to understand that I must be in love and express love to all. To be *in* love is to abide there, to fully comprehend its nature. In love we view the outer scene from above the activity without becoming emotionally involved. Free from those pulls, we can see what is needed and be a harmonizing influence.

My encounter with death was infinitely easier because of the emphasis on loving contemplation in my life since that night of instruction. My prayers and meditations, whether with a group or alone, always begin by focusing awareness on the heart center and feeling the love, then moving into it. So when my heart stopped that December day, I just slipped right into that luminous blue sea of love-light we call God. When we let love smooth the path in life, the moment of our transition is made with ease.

Those who have gone across and come back know that love is the heart and soul of this glorious spiritual renaissance now beginning to shine on earth. Dr. George Ritchie wrote of his death experience as a young soldier. He concludes his book, *Return from Tomorrow*, with this statement: "God is busy building a race of men who know how to love. I believe that the fate of earth itself depends on the progress we make— and that the time now is very short. As for what we'll find in the next world, here too I believe that what we'll discover there depends on how well we get on with the business of loving, here and now."[10]

I was given a second chance at life, and I'm delighted to be here in physical form at this time participating in the great awakening. Hopefully my experience of leaving this world, visiting the other side, and returning to write about it, will help others transcend the fear of death. And I gladly welcome the opportunity to contribute to a greater understanding of what it means to live with love and joy, and to serve in every way I can to help us reach that critical mass of spiritual consciousness in this world. Then, as the Dead Sea Scriptures tell us, "Streaks of lightning will flash from one end of the world to the other, growing ever brighter until the era of darkness is brought utterly to an end."

The spiritual renaissance is indeed upon us; a new light has dawned, an awakening of consciousness brought on in no small measure by the proof of life after death.

Epilogue

On December 30, 1994, I was back in the air again. But instead of riding in a helicopter, this time I was on Continental Flight 1133 to Seattle.

John and I checked our watches occasionally, remembering that day a year before. At about 1:35—the time the near-death experience began—I looked at him and smiled. He took my hand and held it tightly. And a few minutes later I asked, "Am I on the helicopter yet?"

"In about two minutes," he said.

Maybe we had to relive part of that day to bring about a final closure.

Then on the morning of December 31st, at noon Greenwich time (four A.M. on the West Coast), we joined close to a thousand people at the Unity Church in Seattle for the World Healing Meditation. Together we spoke those powerful words, just as I had done alone the year before while in intensive care: "Let peace come forth in every mind ... let love flow forth from every heart ... let forgiveness reign in every soul ... let understanding be the common bond."

We did it for the joy of it, and my unceasing prayer continues to be, "May everyone in the world be happy."

Notes

1: Not an Ordinary Kind of Day

1. *Heart Attack*, American Heart Association, Dallas, Texas, 1989, 1992, 1993.

2: My Husband Remembers

1. Robert Brumet, *Finding YourSelf in Transition* (Unity Village, Mo.: Unity Books, 1995), p. 45.

3: Where It All Began

1. Kenneth Wapnick, *Forgiveness and Jesus* (Roscoe, N.Y.: Foundation for "A Course in Miracles," 1983), pp. 26, 27.
2. Rebecca Ruter Springer, *Intra Muros* (Forest Grove, Ore.: Book Searchers, n.d.), pp. 103–106.

4: The Love Connection

1. Harold Richter Stark, *A Doctor Goes to Heaven* (Boerne, Tex.: Quartus Books, 1982), p. 6.

2. Joseph Campbell, *The Power of Myth* (New York: Doubleday, 1988), p. 75.

3. Manly P. Hall, *The Secret Teachings of All Ages* (Los Angeles: The Philosophical Research Society, Inc., 1977), p. 92.

4. Valerie Moolman, *The Meaning of Your Dreams* (New York: Castle Books, 1969), p. 97.

5. Ken Carey, *Flat Rock Journal* (San Francisco: Harper San Francisco, 1994), p. 230.

6. Michael Talbot, *The Holographic Universe* (New York: HarperCollins Publishers, 1991), p. 245.

7. Ibid., p. 259.

8. Alice A. Bailey, from the writings of, compiled by a student, *Ponder on This* (New York: Lucis Publishing Company, 1971), p. 50.

9. Hall, *Secret Teachings of All Ages*, p. 52.

10. Ibid., p. 83.

11. Emanuel Swedenborg, *The Divine Love and the Divine Wisdom* (New York: Swedenborg Foundation, Inc., 1949), p. 64.

5: *Perceptions of Reality*

1. George G. Ritchie, *Return from Tomorrow* (Old Tappan, N.J.: Spire Books, Fleming H. Revell Company, 1978), p. 51.

2. Rebecca Ruter Springer, *Intra Muros*, p. 119.

3. John Randolph Price, *The Planetary Commission* (Boerne, Tex.: Quartus Books, 1984), pp. 77–78.

4. Ritchie, *Return from Tomorrow*, p. 64.

6: *In the Celestial Silence*

1. Harold Richter Stark, *A Doctor Goes to Heaven* pp. 7, 9, 10.

8: A Look at Death

1. John Randolph Price, *The Angels Within Us* (New York: Fawcett Columbine, Ballantine Books, 1993), p. 185.

2. *A Course in Miracles*, vol. 3, Manual for Teachers (Tiburon, Calif.: Foundation for Inner Peace, 1975), p. 63.

3. *The Sacred Books and Early Literature of the East*, vol. 2, Egypt, with an Historical Survey and Descriptions by Prof. Charles F. Horne, Ph.D. (New York: Parke, Austin, and Lipscomb, 1917), p. 155.

4. Manly P. Hall, *The Secret Teachings of All Ages*, p. 29.

5. *San Antonio (Tex.) Express News*, Jan. 10, 1995, section E, p. 10.

6. Alice A. Bailey, *Esoteric Healing* (New York: Lucis Publishing Company, 1953), p. 394.

7. Alice A. Bailey, *A Treatise on White Magic* (New York: Lucis Publishing Company, 1967), p. 494.

8. Ibid.

9. *Metaphysical Bible Dictionary* (Unity Village, Mo.: Unity School of Christianity, 1931), p. 178.

10. Earlyne Chaney, *The Mystery of Death and Dying* (York Beach, Maine: Samuel Weiser, Inc., 1988), pp. 118, 119.

11. Ernest Holmes, *The Science of Mind* (New York: Dodd, Mead and Company, 1938), p. 478.

12. Manly P. Hall, *The Phoenix* (Los Angeles: Hall Publishing Co., 1931), p. 27.

13. Ibid., p. 23.

14. George W. Meek, *After We Die, What Then?* (Franklin, N.C.: Metascience Corporation, 1980), p. 119.

15. Joseph Campbell, *The Power of Myth* (New York: Doubleday, 1988), p. 56.

16. Alice A. Bailey, *Esoteric Healing*, p. 653.

17. Elizabeth Harper Neeld, *Seven Choices* (New York: Clarkson N. Potter, Inc., 1990), pp. 6, 7.

18. Rodney Collin, *The Theory of Celestial Influence* (Boulder, Colo.: Shambhala Publications, Inc., 1984), pp. 305, 306.

9: Life Continues

1. *The Woodrew Update*, a S.T.A.R. Foundation publication, Jan.–Feb. 1995, p. 5.

2. *The Quartus Report*, vol. ix, no. 2 (Boerne, Tex.: The Quartus Foundation, 1990), p.12.

3. John Randolph Price, *Practical Spirituality* (Boerne, Tex.: Quartus Books, 1985), pp. 82, 83.

10: Cracks in the Veil

1. Manly P. Hall, *The Phoenix*, p. 23.

2. Ibid., p. 26.

3. Ibid.

4. Ibid.

5. From an article by Allen Spraggett, reprinted in *The Quartus Report*, vol. v, no. 4 (Boerne, Tex.: The Quartus Foundation, 1986), p. 12.

6. *The Quartus Report*, vol. ix, no. 3 (Boerne, Tex.: The Quartus Foundation, 1990), p. 9.

7. John Randolph Price, *Angel Energy: How to Harness the Power of Angels in Your Everyday Life* (New York: Ballantine Books, 1995), pp. 192–193.

8. *Guideposts*, published monthly by Guideposts Associates, Carmel, N.Y., Apr. 1994 issue.

11: Memories and Understanding

1. John White, *A Practical Guide to Death and Dying* (Wheaton, Ill.: The Theosophical Publishing House, 1980), p. 153.

2. John Randolph Price, *The Superbeings* (New York: Fawcett Crest, Ballantine Books, 1988).

3. Newton Dillaway, ed., *The Gospel of Emerson* (Wakefield, Mass.: The Montrose Press, 1949), p. 3.

4. Ibid., p. 10.

5. Ibid., p. 16.

6. Ibid., p. 30.

7. Ibid., p. 32.

8. Susan Smith Jones, *Choose to Live Each Day Fully* (Berkeley, Calif.: Celestial Arts, 1994), p. 1.

9. Tom Johnson, *You Are Always Your Own Experience* (Woodland Hills, Calif.: Pathway Enterprises, 1977), p. 30.

12: Bless Your Heart

1. From a condensation of *The Laughter of God*, by Walter C. Lanyon (Inspiration House Publishers, Lees Summit, Mo.) in the June 1994 issue of *Unity* magazine, published by Unity School of Christianity.

13: The Beloved Old Friends

1. Newton Dillaway, ed., *The Gospel of Emerson* (Wakefield, Mass.: The Montrose Press, 1949), p. 29.

2. *The Quartus Report*, vol. xiii, no. 6 (Boerne, Tex.: The Quartus Foundation, June 1994), p. 2.

3. VITVAN, *The Natural Order Process*, vol. 1 (Baker, Nev.: School of the Natural Order, Inc., 1968), pp. 27, 28.

4. Gary Zukav, *Seat of the Soul* (New York: Simon and Schuster, 1989), p. 239.

5. Ibid., p. 89.

6. John Randolph Price, *Empowerment* (Boerne, Tex.: Quartus Books, 1992), p. 73.

14: Rebirth of the Soul

1. Ruth Montgomery, *Here and Hereafter* (New York: Fawcett Crest, Ballantine Books, 1968), p. 10.

2. Emogene S. Simons, *Introductory Study Course in Theosophy* (Wheaton, Ill.: The Theosophical Society in America, 1967), p. 48.

3. Ruth Montgomery, *Here and Hereafter*, pp. 10, 11.

4. Emogene S. Simons, *Introductory Study Course in Theosophy*, p. 48.

5. Bob Larson, *Larson's Book of Cults* (Wheaton, Ill.: Tyndale House Publishers, Inc., 1984), p. 53.

6. Alice A. Bailey, *Esoteric Psychology I* (New York: Lucis Publishing Company, 1967), p. 300.

7. Richard Bach, *The Bridge Across Forever* (New York: William Morrow and Company, Inc., 1984), p. 302.

15: A Spiritual Renaissance

1. As reported by Carol Wright, "Taking Death Lightly," *NAPRA Trade Journal*, Fall 1994, pp. 32–33.

2. *A Course in Miracles*, vol. 1, Text (Tiburon, Calif.: Foundation for Inner Peace, 1975), p. 388.

3. Ibid., p. 391.

4. Emmet Fox, *Power Through Constructive Thinking* (New York: Harper and Row Publishers, 1932), p. 267.

5. Louis Pauwels and Jacques Bergier, *The Morning of the Magicians* (New York: A Scarborough Book, Stein and Day, 1983), p. 70.

6. Newton Dillaway, ed., *The Gospel of Emerson* (Wakefield, Mass.: The Montrose Press, 1949), p. 8.

7. Ibid., p. 37.

8. John Randolph Price, *The Superbeings* (New York: Fawcett Crest, Ballantine Books, 1988), p. 3.

9. Pauwels and Bergier, *Morning of the Magicians*, p. 288.

10. George G. Ritchie, *Return from Tomorrow* (Old Tappan, N.J.: Spire Books, Fleming H. Revell Company, 1978), p. 124.

ABOUT THE AUTHOR

Jan Price is the president and CEO of the Quartus Foundation, a spiritual research and communications organization that she and her husband, John, formed in 1981. The foundation is currently headquartered in Boerne, Texas, near San Antonio.

While this is her first book, Jan is a regular columnist for the magazine *Whole Health*, and has written numerous articles for *The Quartus Report* and other publications. She has also collaborated with John in the writing of twelve inspirational books.

She is an internationally known speaker on the dynamics of positive living and has produced several audiocassette tapes for meditation—and on other such topics as loving yourself, the child within, and the power of at-one-ment. She is the workshop leader for "Freedom Flights"—the personal-growth intensives that she planned and developed—and she shares the platform with John on other seminars and workshops, including the annual Mystery School sponsored by Quartus.

In recognition of their work, Jan and John were presented with The Light of God Expressing Award by the Association of Unity Churches in 1986.

The Prices currently live in the Texas hill country with their dogs, Maggi and Casey.